C000285071

WORK
IT OUT
WITH
A PENCIL

WORK IT OUT WITH A PENCIL

Outrageous Tales from Twenty
Years as an Accountant

TIMOTHY TIMPKINS

Copyright © 2015 by Timothy Timpkins.

Library of Congress Control Number:		2015910032
ISBN:	Hardcover	978-1-5144-6128-0
	Softcover	978-1-5144-6127-3
	eBook	978-1-5144-6129-7

All rights reserved. No part of this book may be reproduced or transmitted in any form or by any means, electronic or mechanical, including photocopying, recording, or by any information storage and retrieval system, without permission in writing from the copyright owner.

Any people depicted in stock imagery provided by Thinkstock are models, and such images are being used for illustrative purposes only. Certain stock imagery © Thinkstock.

Print information available on the last page.

Rev. date: 06/26/2015

To order additional copies of this book, contact:
Xlibris
800-056-3182
www.Xlibrispublishing.co.uk
Orders@Xlibrispublishing.co.uk
709642

CONTENTS

INTRODUCTION

Sitting here writing this foreword and reflecting on over twenty years in an office environment, having worked across numerous roles in accountancy and finance for a variety of companies in several industries, it brings about many different feelings. The most dominant of which is how old I now am and feel as well as how it seems barely half of that time since I first stepped into an office as a paid employee. However, there are also other feelings and memories, good and bad, which have involved both laughter and tears and which, without a doubt, have helped shape me into the person I am today.

The following pages bring some of those stories to life, and I feel they should be shared for two reasons. Firstly, I feel that they are funny and interesting stories (I guess ultimately you will be the judge of that); secondly, if I can prove to just one individual that not all accountants are grey-suited, number-obsessed tax table–loving bores, then I will count that as quite an accomplishment.

For me, no other department within a business seems to attract as many nicknames as finance. The usual ones tend to be bean counters, number crunchers, and number jugglers, to name but three. In over twenty years, I cannot name more than one or two nicknames for any other department of a company, and even then, they never seem to stick for long. Accountants are often seen as the scourge of a business, the negative voice in the room advocating "Why spend a penny when a halfpenny will do?" We're seen as misers, unwilling to spend company money ("treating it as their own" is another common accusation that I personally feel should be a practice more commonplace in business in order to discourage reckless and unnecessary spending) and sucking out all the positive vibes regarding any potentially new and exciting business opportunity due to our perceived negative attitudes. What people tend to forget is that finance is a service department; accountants are there to advise the business on financial matters and the best way forward, from both a financial and finance law perspective. They are also there to help manage business risk and to safeguard a company against potential situations from recent history that companies such as Enron have found themselves in.

For the record, the names of employees and businesses within this book have been either altered or omitted to ensure that former colleagues and current friends are spared any embarrassment, as well as to avoid breaking any confidentiality agreements or finding myself in breach of the Official Secrets Act. I have also embellished some stories slightly – but purely for comedic effect. I hope you find that the book gives a humorous insight into office life, especially for readers who may have never experienced it. I also hope that some of the stories strike a chord with readers who have or do work in accountancy or any other type of office environment on an everyday basis.

CHAPTER 1

The Cheque Run

My first paid role in an office wasn't as daunting for me as it might be for many other eighteen-year-olds who are fresh out of school. They're put into the adult world, away from the security of their friends and the routines they have known for most of their lives. However, I'd already worked in this particular office during the previous month or so as part of my sixth-form business and finance qualification. A permanent role had been advertised within the company, and I was fortunate enough to be in the right place at the right time. Having clearly shown enough promise during my stay so far, I was offered the job. The fact that it was also a ten-minute walk from my parents' house was an added bonus.

The role (trainee accounts assistant) was a newly created one; the finance manager wanted to bring in a bright young individual to spend three months in each area of the department (payroll, cashier, and so forth), learning the ropes, creating a how-to document, and teaching some of the old dogs new tricks when it came to computers. This meant that during peak holiday times or sickness absences, I was there to plug any gaps. My manuals would be available for others to use as easy-to-follow guides, showing what was required in a particular role. What I gained from this job was a two-year grounding in all things finance, which was to put me in good stead in the future. It was a great idea, and I was expected to be the first of many appointments in this position. The department had several staff members reaching retirement age, so it aimed to attract keen young types fresh out of school or college into junior roles, whilst offering progression to existing staff into the more senior positions that would become available in the near to midterm future. Unfortunately, the business began struggling financially so the strategy changed, and ultimately no one followed in my footsteps.

During my first full summer, I was covering a holiday absence in the purchase ledger department. It was a hot, sunny Friday. I always loved Fridays back then, as they meant a 3.30 p.m. finish instead of the usual 5.00 p.m., and the fact that the sun was out meant that my mind was on the first beer of the weekend with my then-girlfriend and some mates. Perhaps what it should have been on was the cheque run I was responsible for. At that time, cheques were still very much in use, as bank transfers were still a bit of a novelty. My company only used transfers in one-off situations, to pay big clients, such as TV marketing companies, on short payment terms. My task was to feed the box of printed company cheques into what was known as the burster machine. This device removed the punch-holed edges from the cheques as well as cut each cheque and remittance (which provided details to the payee of which invoices were being settled within the cheque value) from the next. This way, some poor sod (which invariably at that time would have turned out to be me) would not have to manually separate each one at the perforations.

It was the end of the month, so the number of cheques was well into three figures, so much so that a fresh box of cheques had been opened and affixed to the existing box using sticky tape to allow one big printing run to take place. With the burster in full flow, I was chatting to one of the accountants about his weekend plans whilst bemoaning the tedious task of having to stuff all these cheques into envelopes, seal them, and then stamp them in the post room. It was then that my ears picked up an unusual sound from the machine. Sadly, I had become so accustomed to this machine that I could notice this whilst in full conversation with somebody. It was only when I saw that the cheques were appearing on top of the remittances (they were meant to be below) that panic began to set in and the realisation of the situation dawned on me. I'd forgotten to separate the two parts of the cheque run that had been held together with the sticky tape. The machine was unable to cut at the correct point and instead proceeded to cut at the next perforation, resulting in company A's cheque being attached to company B's remittance and so on for the better part of about fifty cheques.

I managed to stop the machine after what seemed like an age of being rooted to the spot, stunned. The ensuing chaos brought a great deal of attention from the rest of the office, and the ratio of amusement to concern or level of assistance from my colleagues was in no way favourable towards me. I scrambled about pulling at levers and pushing at buttons in the idiotic hope that this would somehow make the problem resolve itself.

Having created two piles of cheques on my desk – to separate those that had been through the machine and were okay from the cheques that would need correcting – I started the machine again to complete the rest of the cheque run. It quickly became obvious that there was a further problem: in my initial panic, I had misaligned the edging part of the machine that removed the punch-holed sides of the cheques, to the extent that it was now taking about a quarter of an inch from each of the remaining cheques. I quickly hit the stop button again, let out a sort of groaning/wailing noise, and desperately looked for either a hole to jump into or for the hidden camera crew that were recording this hilarious prank. Unfortunately for me, neither of these materialised.

This further disruption attracted more attention from the rest of the office, who came to see what the next crisis was – their laughter having only just subsided from the previous one. Luckily, the damage was only to a handful of cheques and was not critical enough to render them useless. I reconfigured the settings on the machine, and it finished the task without further incident. Understandably, I watched it like a hawk until it was complete, which seemed like an eternity.

By this time, it was close to my usual clocking-off time of 3.30 p.m., but I took the decision to stay until every cheque had been corrected and posted out. This was partly due to my growing sense of responsibility and professionalism but mainly a result of my colleagues' position of "You got yourself into this mess; you get yourself out of it." So I sat with what may be the first and only known cheque-repair kit (stapler, scissors, sticky tape) and set about my task whilst the rest of the department gradually left for the day, wishing me a happy weekend and a smug "Don't stay too long!" through the tears of laughter running down their faces.

At about 5.15 p.m., the finance manager emerged from his office, ready to drive home and begin his weekend. He did a double take when he saw that he wasn't the last one in the office for once. He did another one when he saw that it was me, of all people, who was still there. He'd been in meetings with the managing director all afternoon and was oblivious to the carnage that had taken place. Embarrassed, I spent the next five minutes explaining the reason for my presence so late on such a fabulous summer Friday. When I finished, he said two things to me: "Well, I've never known us to have to send out cheques with assembly instructions before," and then he wished me a nice weekend before adding, "And don't think for one minute that you will be getting overtime for this."

CHAPTER 2

On the Buses

The reality that I would not be spending the whole of my working life at the company that first employed me was becoming ever clearer. Rumours of the site closing were occurring more and more frequently, and many of the team were jumping ship for pastures new, often replaced by people who seemed inferior to their predecessors. Many of the original team who remained were beginning to encourage me to seek my future elsewhere, sensing that the writing was indeed on the wall. The majority of those offering such advice didn't appear to be practising what they were preaching. This may have been because they had worked there for over twenty years and were keen to secure what they felt would be well-earned payoffs before seeking their own fresh opportunities.

I attended a small number of job interviews, mainly at other manufacturing companies in the area, but for whatever reason, nothing came of them. I remember one company that was trying to replace a junior accountant who had been doubling up as its information technology guru. It soon became clear that the hirers were hoping for a like-for-like replacement, which struck me as suggesting the company was either being incredibly naive or, worse still, cheap. As my IT knowledge in terms of networks and so forth was rather limited, I was not surprised to receive no response after the interview. I wasn't exactly heartbroken by this, although I do feel that feedback is always nice, as it helps to ensure that you continue to learn from your interview experiences.

Shortly after, I was invited to interview for a job working in the public transport industry; this would give me access to a different industry as well as a job role that would further my accountancy experience substantially. I arrived in good time for the interview. It was late summer, so I was struggling to keep myself cool ahead of meeting the interview panel (no air conditioning in my car back then). I didn't want to appear to be sweating due to nerves, so I got out of the car to take advantage of what little breeze was blowing.

I noticed that the office block was surrounded by houses apart from where the car park backed up to a plot of land that contained a huge amount of bricks and assorted rubble (I later found out that this was the remnants of the company's old garage). I became quite nervous about this, as the office was situated in one of the roughest parts of town. I didn't particularly fancy running a gauntlet of missiles from the local children on days when boredom was getting the better of them. I then looked up to my right to discover that this was proving to be such a day, but fortunately for me, they were busying themselves with dragging some of the heavier items of rubble up an embankment in order to literally lay them across a railway line in the name of fun!

Moving inside to the reception area, I announced who I was and why I was there and then urged the receptionist to contact the police, explaining to her what I had just witnessed. I admit that I found her not-in-the-least-bit-surprised reaction to this news rather disconcerting but tried my best to put it to the back of my mind in order to concentrate on the interview ahead.

I thought that the interview went well, and the relief I felt that I had not appeared completely useless to the three-man panel was multiplied when I returned to my car to find no dents or broken windows and, even better, that all four wheels were still attached so that I would be able to drive home.

Within a week or so, I received the news that I had been offered the position. Despite the potential perils of the car park and interaction with the locals, I accepted the role because it was becoming ever clearer that my current employers were moving towards site closure. Moreover, I wished to experience the greater responsibility and salary that the role afforded me. I was given a nice send-off by the team, many of whom remarked that I was moving from a business that could operate a "carry on accounting" style (as in the 'Carry On' British film franchise) to "on the buses" (a reference to a popular British comedy from the 1960's), but I must admit to feeling a little emotional at saying goodbye to my first place of employment, despite the fact that I knew deep down that it was the right thing to do.

I settled into my new role quite quickly. I was to carry out the reporting for all of the North-based sections of the business whilst Gary, my new colleague, was already doing the same for the South-based areas. Gary was a little older than I was, but we had football and a few other interests in common and got on well with each other as well as with senior accountants Martin and Terry. Gary is still a good friend of mine to this day, and we meet to catch up whenever I'm back in the region. It was important that I got to grips with my new duties quickly, as Gary's fiancée, Debbie, was due to give birth to their first child in a couple of months or so, meaning I would need to cover the majority of Gary's work as well as my own whilst he was on paternity leave.

Gary's politics were, and still very much are, as right wing as it is possible to be without growing a silly little moustache and holding your right arm up a lot, if you get my meaning. He was unequivocal in his praise for Margaret Thatcher and, equally, his hatred for trade unions and their beliefs; any news stories that concerned people protesting or rioting would always result in Gary calling for the police to send the horses in, preferably with tear-gas canisters and water cannons.

A few weeks into the job, we were still being blessed by a late summer heatwave. The office windows were open wide to try to gain whatever breeze we could, given the office was so old and the company so tight-fisted that there was no air conditioning available. Before long, we could hear the voices of a handful of local children playing football in the lane between the office and some houses. In a matter of minutes, the football was booted through an open window and into our office on the top floor, ricocheting across several desks and knocking cups and paperwork into the air. Putting this down to an accident, we returned the ball with a request for the children to be more careful.

By the time the ball had cannoned around our office for the fourth time, it was obvious that this was the whole objective of these little angels. Having had enough, Gary retrieved the ball and launched it back towards the group, smashing one of them full in the face. Unconcerned by his actions, Gary then announced, "If you little bastards don't stop it, I will pour a bucket of hot piss over you!" Where Gary intended to procure such an item was not obvious to me, and it seemed that all the others in the office were in too much of a state of shock by what they had just witnessed to investigate this further with him. Incredibly, this seemed to do the trick, as the remainder of the afternoon passed without incident.

Such incidents were quite commonplace, which was unsurprising to me given the area that we were located in; the area is still very deprived and contains a high proportion of unemployed and those reliant on benefits.

Gary and I would regularly take a stroll at lunchtime to stretch our legs and get away from our desks, and it was virtually guaranteed that we would see something or someone out of the ordinary. This was always particularly useful in offering a sense of grounding to Gary and me if we had been cursing the fact that we had a poor way of life or were bemoaning our jobs.

Particular highlights for me during these lunchtime excursions include seeing one of the unemployed masses sunning himself on a 1970s sun recliner that he had decided to situate between two parked cars in his street.

On another occasion, we were walking past a house that was well known for being operated as a brothel (believe me, there was absolutely nothing discreet about this place) just as two of the "ladies" were struggling to carry a wheelchair bound regular up the stairs to their place of business. I seem to remember Gary and I being too stunned by this spectacle to even consider helping the girls. Besides, we would then have felt duty-bound to wait until he needed carrying back down, and neither of us wanted to do that or have to try to explain to Martin and Terry the reason for our being late back from lunch.

Without a doubt, the craziest thing that we witnessed was on an autumn day. We weren't long into our usual walking route when a young man in his mid-teens dashed past us, almost knocking us both to the ground. By the time we had gathered our composure and finished shouting complaints at him, we were confronted by about a dozen or so teenage boys, all running towards us and brandishing mallets! Fortunately for us, they raced past and continued their pursuit of the first teenager; we simply carried on with our walk in a state of utter bemusement at the fact that we assumed we had seen it all but this area just kept on surprising us.

Before long, it was becoming obvious to me that whilst the level of work I was carrying out was a step up from my previous role and involved my having to undertake more regularly monthly reporting and interaction with areas such as value added tax and national statistic returns, the company were not in the habit of speculating money to accumulate money (although it appears that this strategy has altered somewhat in recent years). They were operating in a market where there was seemingly an acceptance of the fact that revenues would continually shrink in the years ahead – without any obvious strategies forthcoming as to what was being considered to counteract this.

The head office was based in the city centre and had an iconic view, and I can honestly say that during the whole of my time there, I could easily count on one hand the number of visits that members of the board made to our office. Don't get me wrong – I didn't need a chief executive to walk the office floor to get me motivated, and I'm sure some of the stories I have detailed in this chapter would provide a decent argument as to why they may have been avoiding the place at all costs. However, I think it's important that business leaders engage with their staff at least two to four times a year, if only to prove that they don't just sit in their ivory towers, locked away from the realities that the majority of the employees of the business are facing. I'd even known some business executives to join employees in the designated smoking areas, as it was sometimes the best way to find out what was happening day to day or to gauge the mood among the workforce.

What I also found ridiculous was the fact that the head office was clearly too small and poorly equipped but it was said that the chief executive was refusing to consider relocating, as his office "had a great view". Additional office space and furniture could have been rented within the building they already occupied, but that was deemed an unnecessary expense, despite the fact that Gary and I were aware of a colleague who worked there that was being forced to use two cardboard boxes for a desk! (One week he had to share this arrangement with a young guy who had joined to carry out some work experience. Quite what the student made of this as his first taste of office life is unknown, but as far as I was aware, he showed no appetite to return once his education was complete).

It also never ceased to amaze me how tactless the management could appear towards the workforce, although I would suggest that in most cases (or perhaps all) it was unintentional. I can remember Chris Kirk, a hard-working operations manager and a man I liked and respected, making the decision to attend a meeting with the workforce and their unions to refute their pay demands in his brand-new metallic gold Mercedes! To me, this seemed a ridiculous idea from a guy who generally struck me as being quite smart, especially as the workforce already saw him as being somewhat of a flash git due to his sharp suits and Bee Gees–like gleaming teeth. The meeting proceeded and was concluded without incident, whereas Gary and I were expecting to hear stories of Chris sitting in his new car while an angry mob of our best blue-collar workers rocked it back and forth, trying to get him out to remove those perfect pearly white teeth of his.

Having spent roughly two and a half years in my role in the public transport industry, I started to get the feeling that it was time to move on again, although this time there was no real threat of redundancy or site closure. It was more about the fear of boredom gripping me and the realisation that I could quite easily take two days away from the office and return knowing that there would be no backlog of work for me to tackle. I had also made Martin aware of my desire to take on more challenging additional tasks, only to be told that there would be nothing forthcoming. I was in the position where I could carry out my current role standing on my head until retirement, so stagnation was proving to be a very real prospect. There appeared to be little chance of progression either, given that the people above me were a mixture of being nowhere near retirement age and seemingly incredibly unambitious. I found myself regularly having that conversation with both my fiancée and Gary, who was also feeling more than a little underutilised. Gary was also growing tired of having to wear a company tie to work, mainly as he regularly used the company's transport service as part of his commute and would be hounded regularly by other passengers wanting an explanation as to why the service was late or slow or why a certain route had been changed or removed.

One memory of this time that is still vivid in my mind is of Gary and me sitting at our desks one Monday morning. The only guaranteed work we had for the entire week was just one bus depot petty cash return each. Martin had confirmed that he, Terry, and the finance director had no tasks which they wanted us to carry out or assist them with, so Gary and I did the most rigorous audit of our petty cash returns imaginable. We cross-checked values, ensured that all receipts had VAT numbers on them, and checked that VAT values against the return were correct and appropriate according to the latest tax rules. Somehow we managed to spin this task out to the best part of an hour, but given that it was still only ten o'clock on Monday morning and no further work had materialised, we did the only thing possible and swapped petty cash returns to cross-check each other's workings. This managed to kill another hour of the day. We somehow made it to five o'clock by spending most of the rest of the day making copious amounts of tea and coffee for the office as well as brushing up on the latest fire regulations (months earlier, Chris Kirk and I had been "volunteered" for fire marshalling duties for the office).

Luckily, work picked up later in the week, but not before we found ourselves with enough time to establish the best escape route from the office should a crazed gunman burst through the main entrance. (For the record, Gary would have made an attempt for the fire escape some ten yards south-east of his desk, whilst I personally would have opted for jumping out of the window next to me, which would have been a risky strategy given that we weren't situated on the ground floor.)

I began contacting recruiters to make my availability known; the security of the role I was carrying out was being hugely outweighed by the tediousness of the weeks in the middle of the month with very little to do. I was also becoming more and more convinced that I could find a position with another business that offered a similar or better role but which carried a greatly improved salary. My salary had not grown in line with my experience and the ability I had shown over the course of my employment, as the business tended to be rather frugal with wage rises and instead preferred to offer other incentives such as company share schemes. While this was undoubtedly a good perk, the terms of these schemes dictated that you would need to commit to being part of the company for a minimum of five years in order to achieve the maximum gains from the scheme. I was convinced that from a job satisfaction perspective, I would be unable to do that without losing my sanity first. Also, it appeared to me that many of the others in the office were trapped in their roles due to the amount of money they had invested in these schemes and clearly felt that working in such a mundane job with little prospects and barely adequate pay was a price worth paying for the incentive being offered.

I make no apology for the fact that I was also keen to boost my salary because I now had a mortgage to pay, having decided to buy my own home. This was never really a huge ambition of mine but was borne out of the necessity to move out of the council-owned rental property that I was sharing with my fiancée, for our neighbours were every bit as charming as those at my place of work. At one stage, my fiancée was working three jobs so that we could save enough money for a deposit to allow us to escape the eighteen months of sheer hell we experienced in that house. The continual drinking and partying by our unemployed neighbours was starting to affect our mental state of mind (German techno music was never a favourite of mine beforehand and was even less so after my time at that property). In addition, the incessant vandalism and attempted thefts of our vehicles had led me to the point where I was parking my car at my parents' house and being driven to and from it by both my fiancée and my parents on a daily basis.

As much as I hated my time at that property, it taught me the valuable lesson that I never again wanted to be in a position where I had to live in such a place and that it did not matter how hard I had to work or how many jobs I had to undertake to ensure this.

CHAPTER 3

Job Interviews

Job interviews are never easy. Especially if, like me, you sometimes allow nerves to get the better of you, meaning your enthusiastic responses turn into completely the wrong thing to say in a matter of seconds. In my case, I know this is mainly down to a little overconfidence when things are going well in the interview.

I've attended many interviews over the years, mainly because the job I was in became stale or there was seemingly no further development on the horizon. Also, moving job roles around every two to three years is something accountants tend to do; it allows them to broaden their experiences into different roles and in other industries. Before my last role as an accountant, I never stayed with a business longer than three years – not just for the reasons above but also because I was young and ambitious and keen to earn more money to allow me to pay my mortgage; buy nice things for me, my wife, my family, and friends; and to enjoy a bit of life. Work hard and play hard was very much my mantra and still is to this day.

Inevitably, this leads you into management roles where you attend interviews but the roles are reversed. Now you are the one asking the questions; you are the one having to promote how good it is to work at the company and how attractive the role is and how genuinely helpful everyone in the team is to the nervous, sweaty individual across the desk from you. I never had any sort of interview training in all of my years as a manager, so I had to improvise; my style was to ensure that I treated the candidates in the way I would have wanted to be treated myself. I also made a point of adding some levity early on in interviews in an effort to try to put candidates at ease (as well as myself).

I pride myself on being quite a good judge of character. I've always tended to gravitate towards good people, even back when I was a schoolboy. I arrived at a high school of about two thousand pupils not knowing anyone, but I somehow surrounded myself with the good kids. I can think of only one appointment in my career that I regret which came from my time in the construction industry. I would say that the candidate was in a pool of one, and I took the decision that some help was better than no help. I was wrong. As it transpired, I was to leave the company shortly after this appointment (but not because of it; the reason for my leaving is explained in a later chapter), and the candidate didn't last too much longer after that. His African culture probably counted against him given that he primarily had to deal with some rough-arsed labourers who were not known for their tolerance of those who are different (not the candidate's fault). But he also believed that any female workers, regardless of their roles, were to be treated as nothing more than lowly secretaries and worthy of only being talked to as if they were second-class citizens (very much the candidate's fault).

I was also once guilty of contriving an interview to ensure that the candidate I wanted got the role. I'd moved from construction to the airline industry; my team was one short, so we contacted the recruiters to send in some CVs. I also privately contacted a girl called Toni who had worked for me in my previous role. I knew Toni was looking to leave, as my replacement wasn't endearing himself to anyone in my old team and was proving to be very much the polar opposite of me in terms of management style.

My assistant (and the successful candidate's future supervisor) and I narrowed the CVs down to two people: a young lad currently out of work and Toni. I briefed Toni ahead of her interview of the right things to ask and what strengths to play on. The other candidate was going to have to give the interview of his life to get the job, and whilst that may appear unfair, his CV didn't suggest that this was likely, and I knew from personal experience how good Toni was. Sure enough, Toni came across as the standout candidate. I could sense that my assistant felt that something was not quite above board with Toni but she didn't pursue it. In mitigation, Toni remained at the company long after I had left, even having her redundancy leave date extended numerous times until she pretty much turned out the lights on the place when it finally closed and relocated to the South of the country.

Without doubt, the most outrageous interview process I was ever involved in was when I was looking to make a move out of public transport and into an exciting new role. A recruitment company sent a job description to me for a role with a relatively new manufacturing company in the North. Their workload was increasing, and they needed someone to come in and handle the finance aspects of their small to medium-sized contracts. They also had an American operation and were ultimately owned by a US conglomerate whose chairman would become the vice president of the United States within a year of my interview.

The first interview took place at about six o'clock on a Tuesday night. As anyone who has worked in an office knows, it is quite common for interviews to occur outside of normal hours, as many candidates are already employed and are unlikely to be able to make an interview within the usual nine-to-five office hours without having a good reason for needing to leave their workplaces early. Wearing one's best suit or a sharp new shirt also tends to arouse suspicion amongst current employers and colleagues.

The interview was held in a small meeting room on the ground floor of the office building; the building was quite new and very high tech for the time, with doors that needed a swipe card to allow you to enter. There were few people around other than the accountant and human resources representative who were conducting my interview. I tried to remain calm and not look too nervous. It was going well and I was answering most of the questions with clear, concise responses. I got the impression that the accountant knew a bit about the public transport industry I was describing as my current role (it later turned out that he had worked in the same role for the same company some years before). This was good news for me, as it meant there was an instant affinity between us and proved as well that I wasn't bullshitting or making the role out to be more than it actually was.

The interview concluded with my being shown a sample of their main product. They asked me to describe how I thought it was manufactured. I was hopeless. There is a reason I worked in an office for so long, and that is because I have no manual skills or creative imagination whatsoever. It brings to mind a conversation I had recently with my partner's brother; he is very much an engineering type, and it soon becomes pretty obvious to anyone I meet that I am not. "I bet if you had Legos as a kid, you just copied the build book instead of trying to create your own rocket or car," he said. Sadly, he was correct. Building things using imagination was never my strong point, but I was confident that in the case of the interview question, my pathetic explanation would not have too much of a bearing on the outcome, given that it was ultimately a finance job I was being interviewed for and not that of a design engineer.

With all questions asked and answered and the human resources officer happy with her notes and scribbles, we shook hands and said our goodbyes. They informed me that they would shortlist the candidates down to two or three and a second interview would be held with the finance manager. It was wait and see time. I'm never one to get my hopes up, but I felt I had a good chance for a second interview. Later that week, the recruitment consultant confirmed that the company wanted to see me again. We agreed on an appointment at 6.30 the following Monday night.

Experience tells you that, more often than not, a second interview tends to be an informal chat with the main guy to see if he feels you are someone he likes the look of and can see himself working with. The hard work generally takes place in the first interview, but the second interview can be the point where saying the wrong thing snatches defeat from the jaws of victory for a candidate. Such a pivotal moment was about to transpire for me.

The second interview took place in the same room as the first; the same accountant greeted me, but this time there was no HR representation. It was evident that this guy had decided on the two or three candidates he felt he could work with and that this was about which of us the finance manager liked the look of the most. After a brief wait, the finance manager bounded into the room and was full of introductions and handshakes. We then got down to business. The first question I was asked: "Do you like football and, if so, which team do you support?" As a born and bred northerner, it's always deemed odd to other football fans that my team is not my home town club (in fact, it is Liverpool, as they were the first team I ever saw play – they won easily and became my team, which they still are nearly thirty-five years later). As always, I had to explain the reason for my choice of football team, but I was quickly left in no doubt that "Sunderland" would have been the worst possible answer I could have given.

The next question: "Do you like to drink?" Again, this wasn't on the list of potential questions for which I had prepared myself. However, I also wasn't getting the impression that this guy was some sort of puritan who had a huge issue with anyone who entertained the devilment of alcohol (a theory that was proved correct on many occasions in the years that followed). Again, I got the feeling that a response of no would not have been received too favourably.

Next up was less of a question and more of a threatening statement of fact: "We sometimes have to work late to get the job done or to meet tight deadlines. I hope you're not one of those that, come five o'clock, you're putting your hat and coat on and heading for the exit; otherwise,

I'll be asking you to pick a window." In case anyone is unaware, to "pick a window" suggests that he would be consequently throwing me through it once I'd made my selection. There was just enough of an element of humour behind the words to convince me that this was his light-hearted attempt to assess how much of a team player I was and not a serious threat or common management technique that he regularly employed.

Having asked me if I had any questions and provided his responses to them, he then said, "Following an article I read in a magazine a few days ago, there are two questions that it suggested I should ask to close the interview. So here goes: what one question did you dread being asked today?" With the thought of my first interview, and the poor description I had offered of how the main product was manufactured still fresh in my mind, I responded that I had been concerned about being asked anything technical like that.

"OK, the final question is … can you tell me a joke?" I had never before or since been asked such a question, and as final interview questions go, it is an absolute beauty because no matter how well things have gone up to that point, all your hard work can be completely obliterated by misjudging this. I'd known this guy barely fifteen minutes and the other interviewer for about half an hour longer than that, so to ask me to pitch this at their sense of humour (making the assumption that they had a similar sense of humour) was not going to be easy at all.

I thought quickly and had only two jokes in my mind that I'd recently been told (incidentally, both by my mother). My audience waited expectantly to be amused (at that moment, I would have been happy just to ensure that they weren't insulted or offended), so I had to choose quickly. The first joke involved the Norse god Thor visiting Earth and proving his greatness by chatting up a woman and having a one-night stand with her. The next morning, worrying that he may have been overenthusiastic during sex, he apologised to her and explained, "I'm Thor." She replied, "You're Thor? I can't even pith!" Now, granted, this is far from being one of the world's greatest jokes, but its quality was not my main concern. What if the finance manager's wife had a speech

23

impediment! I could blow all of my hard work by telling this joke. So having ruled it out and weighing up the fact that I seemed to be in front of two men of the world, I opted for the other joke that was fresh in my mind. To this day, I still don't know where I found the audacity to tell it or why I ever thought it would be suitable in any environment other than a stag party, never mind a job interview.

The joke goes like this: One Sunday morning a man and his wife are lying in bed. It's a beautiful day, and he suggests that they and their dog go fishing. She's not keen and can't be talked around but concedes to go the following Sunday if the weather is just as good. When the next Sunday comes around, it's another great day. Reminding his wife of her promise, the husband suggests that they and their dog head out fishing. Once again, she's not keen but assures her husband that next week they will definitely go. On the following Sunday, they wake up to another gorgeous day; the husband reminds his wife of her promise, but yet again, she is not keen to leave her nice warm bed. "OK," says the husband, "if you, me, and the dog aren't going fishing, then you have to accept a forfeit of either giving me oral sex or anal sex. I'll give you some time to think it over." When he returns, he asks if she's made a decision. She agrees to give her husband oral sex but within seconds is recoiling and gagging at the taste. "My God, that is disgusting. What have you been doing?" she asks. The husband replies, "Well, the dog didn't want to go fishing either ..."

There was a second of stunned silence before they both started laughing; somehow, via a bestiality joke, I had gotten away with this. As the accountant escorted me out of the room and towards the car park, I noticed a woman sitting at at a desk outside the meeting room. (I later found out that she was the human resources manager. She once commented to me that she had never heard so much laughter in an interview before or since; luckily, she didn't know the reason why, and I was not about to tell her anytime soon.) As I said goodbye and shook hands, I noticed he was still laughing but had a slightly shocked look on his face. I explained that I just felt I had to give it a go; it was some time later that I confessed to them that it was a joke that I had actually heard from my mother! It took about six months before I attended the first team meeting where the finance manager didn't request that I kick things off by telling the team a joke.

CHAPTER 4

Construction

Having spent just over three years in my role in manufacturing, I had once again started to get the feeling that it was time to move on. A previous management regime that was being funded through a venture capital firm had just bought out the company, but again, there was no real imminent feeling of potential job losses or a downturn in orders. It was more about my desire to tackle additional, more challenging tasks. Yet again, there appeared little chance of progression, as the guys above me who had offered me the role despite (or perhaps even because of) *that* joke were not that much older than I was, so they were not making any plans for retirement and seemed happy enough in their current roles to not be considering a move elsewhere in the company or to pastures new. To date this was the longest I had stayed in one role, I was on good terms with almost everyone who worked on the site (there are always exceptions), and whilst my manager had always looked after me salary-wise, the thought of a new challenge was burning within me. I was almost twenty-seven years old and still ambitious; I also had a mortgage, and my fiancée and I were fast developing a taste for travel and the finer things in life, which, coming from humble backgrounds, we would have to fund through progression in our professional careers.

A job role was passed my way by a recruitment agency; it was a management role for a construction firm on the other side of the river. The combination of managing staff and working in an industry I had no experience in was an exciting and attractive prospect to me. I applied and was asked to attend an interview. I was interviewed by the finance director and his assistant (who I later discovered was also his wife but, thankfully, without the embarrassment of having trash-talked to one about the other, which is my usual style of finding these sorts of things out). They operated out of the company head office that was based in the South and had travelled up to conduct the interviews. It became obvious that should I be offered and accept the role that I would be the senior finance person on-site. This appealed immensely to my sense of ambition, and I became even more determined to outline my suitability for the job.

The interview went well, but one line of questioning that struck me as slightly odd was their keenness to understand how firm I could be with the management in matters that I perceived to be potentially in breach of financial standards. I didn't let it put me off the role, and my answers were obviously what they were looking for, for within the week, I was invited for a second interview with the managing director of the business unit. Again, this second interview was to allow the senior manager to assess whether he could build a working relationship with me. Paul, the managing director, was someone who obviously knew the business from top to bottom, and he was remarkably frank about what he expected of his finance manager. "Look, son, I'm going to bend the rules as much as possible and what I want you to do is step in before I break them. Do you think you can do that for me?" Slightly taken aback by the candid nature of his question, I assured him that I was the type of person who was pragmatic enough to realise that not everything is black and white but also someone who had a clear opinion on what was right and wrong. If he could be that frank with me about such things, then I was certain I could ensure that the business remained within the boundaries of what was both morally and legally correct.

It wasn't long before I received the news that the position was mine. I accepted and then broke the news to my current manager; he accepted it with good grace and seemed to understand fully the reasons I was seeking to broaden my horizons. The news didn't go down too well with the finance director, who accused my manager of not trying hard enough to retain me, but in fairness, my mind was made up. My manager sensed that during our discussion and rightly concluded that there was little point in trying to convince me to stay.

My four-week notice period soon ended, and it was decided that I would leave in style. We finished at lunchtime on my last day and headed into the city for a bite to eat and to enjoy the delights of one of the most popular gay bars in town, which, bizarrely, had a female strip show on Friday afternoons. My good friend Gary from my time in public transport made the journey over to join in the festivities. We each handed over our three pounds and headed to the bar for a drink whilst somewhat chauvinistically anticipating exactly what standard of performer we could expect to be entertained with given the rather low entry fee. There was a reasonable crowd, predominantly male obviously and, as far as I could establish, consisting mainly of two types of client: labouring types who had also finished work for the week and dirty old men in macs. The five of us in our group were clearly neither of those, so the venue had unwittingly gained a third demographic for the afternoon.

Whilst it was obvious that the performers were never going to be retired catwalk models, they were proving popular with the crowd. One woman's performance was very interactive with the audience, which, thanks to my friends, meant I was forced to become part of the act, and my assistance was soon required to remove her bra. I have no qualms about admitting that I was nowhere near drunk enough to be anything other than terrified by this prospect, and rather than savouring this moment in the style that some of the other audience members had been doing when called upon to help "Mandy" (her stage name) undress, I carried out my duties with all the speed and panache of a member of a Formula One pit crew.

I began my new role the following Monday, and I was introduced to my new team, which equated to two youngsters (Toni and Tina) and a middle-aged former labourer (Lloyd). Lloyd was carrying out office duties due to a work-related accident he had suffered some months previously. (This was a practice that I discovered was quite commonplace across this business in an effort to keep lost workdays down to an absolute minimum.) It was at this point that I made my first mistake as a manager, as, in my mind, I pencilled in Lloyd as my second in command. This was because he was only a few years younger than my father was, so I presumed that he would possess a similar work ethic and dedication and be able to act as my eyes and ears in the office during my absence, ensuring that Toni and Tina did their fair share of the work. In fact, it transpired that Lloyd was the worst offender of the team when it came to slacking off, and ultimately Toni would become my assistant due to her honesty and willingness to work hard.

Tina soon moved to work at the newly created joint venture, but we weren't short-handed, as a young guy (Mickey) on a twelve month work experience secondment from his university course had been dropped on me. Mickey's girlfriend had an uncle who was a senior figure at the head office and had managed to secure him a year in our business, the only problem being that our site had absolutely no clue what to do with him and had been assigning him such illuminating tasks as photocopying and filing. Having lost Tina to the joint venture and been told to use Mickey, I then found myself having to stop people from periodically requesting his help with such critical tasks like refilling the stationary cupboard. I was thankful for the early opportunity to show that I was not prepared to be pushed around or put up with any shit from others, and I am certain that Mickey was thankful to be given a proper role that he could not only carry out but also improve over the course of his time with us.

I immediately saw the benefit in continuing this type of arrangement once Mickey had returned to university. To me, it was a way of trialling up-and-coming youngsters in a small role with the chance to be first in line for their services should they show enough promise and a desire to work in the finance department of a construction company. It was also cheap labour and meant that any candidates that weren't quite good enough wouldn't affect the business financially and I would be able to reorganise the workload to ensure that the critical work would always be prioritised. Later on, I would also extend this to a local scheme promoting youth apprenticeships, where we could interview sixteen- to eighteen-year-olds and take them on trial for a small weekly fee before deciding whether they were suitable. Those who showed promise would be offered full-time positions, whilst those who didn't were sent back as being not good enough. This was good business, as well as being virtually zero risk, in an industry operating on tiny margins. During my time there, a number of candidates successfully gained full employment with the company through this route.

One of my main duties was to fly to the head office every month with Paul and two of his other management team members, Lenny and Willie, to report the financial results and general performance of the business for the previous month to the main board, which included my finance director. It was usually a return trip within the same day but was further good experience of how to communicate with business leaders.

My first lesson in such a skill occurred within weeks of my first ever job. My manager invited me to attend a meeting that he had scheduled with the managing director. This was to allow me an introduction to the top guy as well as provide a lesson in how the finance department helps the business on a day-to-day basis. The introduction went well, but the lesson certainly didn't go as my manager had planned, as his unequivocal no to a proposal made by the managing director was met by a barrage of bad language before my manager was then chased out of the office in a scene reminiscent of a sketch from an old black-and-white comedy movie. The lesson I learned was to respond to senior management proposals this way: "That may work, but have you considered doing it this way?" To ensure I avoided the almost slapstick scene I had just witnessed, that was preferable to just saying no.

On one of my monthly reporting visits, I remember we had adjourned for lunch; the meeting was going well, and we had managed to answer the queries levelled at us so far, explaining the results quite well. We sat with the chief executive, and he was telling us about his recent holiday in Turkey. Turkey was a particular sore point with Willie, as his politics were very much right wing and he had a particular dislike for the proposal at the time to admit Turkey into the European Union. I could see Willie beginning to line up the conversation towards his usual opinion of being totally against the prospect of allowing twenty million Muslims into the EU. Luckily for Willie, before he could make the point, the chief executive explained that he was a regular visitor to the country due to the fact his wife was Turkish. Willie and I looked at each other and silently recognised just how close he had just come to handing in his resignation in the most creative way possible.

Working in construction certainly put me in contact with a vast array of characters. Without wishing to seem unkind, many manual workers in this industry were not exactly going to appear on *Mastermind* or be at pains to debate the works of the Bronte sisters, but overall, I found them to be down to earth and friendly, if somewhat a little crazy.

One of the site supervisors, a guy called Ernie, was walking out of the office with Mickey and me one evening; I was going to give Mickey a lift home. Ernie asked Mickey if he was going partying that night. Mickey hadn't been with us long and seemed a little unsure as to how to respond, probably because he may have felt an affirmative answer on a "school night" in front of his manager would not be a wise move. "No, Ernie, I'm just staying at home tonight," said Mickey. Ernie replied, "Oh, yes, bashing the bishop instead, are you?" before wishing us a good night and driving off. Now, for those not aware of this turn of phrase, it is most definitely not a chess reference but rather more an insinuation that Mickey would be performing an act of self-indulgence all evening. Mickey and I just looked at each other as if to confirm what we had just heard and then spent the whole journey home with a mixture of bemusement and laughter.

I also remember my office once being the scene of a terrific practical joke. We often employed a consultant called Ed, who spent most of his time on our work sites but from time to time would venture into the office to discuss issues with the senior management. Ed had a great sense of humour and was always good at winding up others; one day he set his sights on a foreman called Dave Dolphin. Ed waited for Dave to leave his desk and placed a note on it that read as follows: *Mr Lyon, 0207 449 6200.* The telephone number that had been written down was for London Zoo. When Dave returned, he came into my office and asked about the message on his desk; I explained that Ed had taken a call and that the caller hadn't stated the nature of the call but that it seemed quite urgent.

We later discovered from Dave that the conversation went something like this: Dave – "Hello, can I speak to Mr Lyon, please?" London Zoo (clearly no stranger to such requests) – "Nah, sorry, mate. He's having his lunch at the minute. Who is this?" Dave (still completely in the dark and being 100 per cent genuine) – "This is Mr. Dolphin. I'm just returning his call from earlier." London Zoo – "Look, pal, we do the fucking jokes around here, OK?" The person from the zoo then slammed the phone down.

Several months into my role, I received an email from my previous manager; the accountant who had interviewed me had decided to leave, and they were wondering if I would like to return to replace him. This was an unexpected turn of events and put me in a huge dilemma. The lack of progression was the main reason for wanting to leave, and now the opportunity had presented itself, but only after I had made a move into a bigger role in a different industry. As tempting as it was to return, I ultimately made the decision to stay where I was, as I always felt that the old adage of "You should never go back" was a good one. However, a business decision in my new company was about to throw doubt on whether I had made the correct decision.

Not long after declining the offer to return to my old employer, my current company made a change in the management team. Paul was to "retire" (only to set himself up as a consultant and ply his trade for the joint venture), and Terry, the general manager, was to take over the role. Terry was someone who, to his credit, had pulled himself up from nothing to be in a position of senior management. He was a hard worker but crucially seemed to be devoid of Paul's style. He was also widely known to push the boundaries of what was legally right, let alone morally. He was a big, imposing figure and wasn't afraid to use this as his primary management technique.

He also had a tendency to contact you at any hour of the day, depending on when he thought of a query. For some reason, he didn't appear to have the ability to store the thought until an appropriate moment. I remember once standing in a supermarket queue waiting to pay for my lunch and receiving several calls from him, despite my assurances that I would be back on-site within five minutes. I sensed that my ability to ensure that financial and legal lines would not be crossed was about to be tested to the limit; this seemed to ring even more true when Lenny, having gotten to the point where his working relationship with Terry was almost non-existent, moved to a role within the joint venture. Terry hand-selected Lenny's replacement, a guy called Graeme, who was recruited from a smaller outside firm rather than internally, a move clearly carried out to ensure that he was under no illusion from Terry as to how operations were to be run day to day.

My first experience of the new order of things came quickly. We were operating on a contract in one of the most destitute areas of the region, and the natives wasted no time in helping themselves to whatever our workers had left on site at the end of the day, securely locked up or otherwise. On one occasion, an overnight delivery of ten tonnes of topsoil had been completely removed in the few hours between delivery and the team arriving for work. The site manager was so impressed by the effort shown by the locals that he was prepared to offer any of the culprits a job on the contract! They were regularly breaking into the site, looking for anything that may hold some value; that even included the metal on the back of signs or anything that could potentially bring them some money to spend on their various vices. The situation got to the point where Graeme would visit the site with a minder as well as a length of pipe hidden up the sleeve of his jacket.

As the contract still had several weeks to run, a meeting was scheduled with the head villain of the area (known locally as the "king of the gypsies") in order to broker a deal that allowed our team to work without fear of violence or the need to clear the site completely at the end of each day. An agreement was reached to pay this individual 150 pounds per week. There was an instant culture change, and the site remained untouched for the rest of the contract. However, my issue with this arrangement was how the transactions would be carried out, which was for Graeme to come to me every week to request 150 pounds from the petty cash tin. In return, he would hand me what was laughably referred to as an invoice for "STIHL saw repairs" from the head villain. When I asked how he thought I would be expected to justify this should it ever come under any sort of scrutiny by an audit team, the response was as I had feared: "Well, that's your department, son."

As the months went on, the stress of trying to contain things inside the rule of financial law grew ever greater as various other schemes were clearly being hatched. I got the impression that my concern at some of the proposals was being viewed by both Graeme and Terry as evidence of my possessing a soft streak. I also felt that they were beginning to shut me out of certain discussions, which meant that I was potentially being placed in a position in which I could not act on something that blurred the lines of financial regulations until it was far too late. I was working longer and longer hours and, as a result, asking more and more of my team. By this time, I had three youngsters working for me. Toni was still there and was very much my right hand, Mickey had gone back to university and had been replaced by another undergraduate called Rob, while Lloyd had accepted a job within the joint venture, mainly due to the fact that I had discovered he was swinging the lead through the week to enable himself to justify working the weekend and supplement his wages. (Rarely were people fired in this business. For some reason, they were always shunted off somewhere else). An apprentice called Ben from the Youth Scheme had replaced him.

I got into the habit of taking the team out every Friday for lunch as a way of thanking them for their efforts and for putting up with my increasing moods in the office, the number of which would vary depending on how much shit I was having to deal with from Graeme and Terry. More often than not, I would pay for the lunches myself, but sometimes Terry would suggest that I take some petty cash to pay for it, as his own way of thanking the team and me.

Before long, our Friday lunch hours were becoming two and a half hours long. We were also drinking several alcoholic drinks over the course of the lunch and, if tested, would have easily failed the company drug and alcohol policy as well as a police breathalyser. I was required to attend a meeting chaired by Terry at three o'clock every Friday, and it continuously amazed me that he never commented on the fact that I stunk of alcohol or wondered why I was excusing myself to visit the toilet every fifteen minutes.

I am not proud of my behaviour during this time in my life. It fills me with shame that I was prepared to put not only my own life at risk but also that of my team, not to mention pedestrians and other road users, due to my own thoughtless, irresponsible actions. It is in no way an excuse, but upon reflection, I am convinced that the pressure of my working week was clearly taking its toll and this was my way of dealing with it.

The point where I realised something had to be done for the sake of my own health came when Graeme asked me to effectively carry out a spying role on a site supervisor of ours called Freddie. This did not sit comfortably with me at all. Besides, I liked Freddie, as he was a decent guy who clearly saw Graeme as a chancer and by now had absolutely no working relationship with him. I decided to go speak with Terry about this. Despite the fact that he and Freddie were also not on good terms due to a falling out at a function months earlier over an incident where Freddie tried to throw peanuts into Terry's open mouth whilst he was comatose from alcohol, I was sure that the hard work and commitment I had given to Paul, Terry, and Graeme for almost two years would count for something.

It turned out I was wrong, for instead of backing me, Terry thought Graeme's proposal was a good one and said he would appreciate it if I would carry out the request in full. Looking back, I'm surprised by how sure I was that Terry would appreciate my reservations on doing as I'd been asked. Graeme was his man, hand-picked to carry out his wishes, whereas ultimately I had been thrust upon him without choice and had always been in the position of having two managers, Terry and the finance director, a fact that Terry made no attempt to hide his frustration about.

With what I saw as a slap in the face for all my efforts, I went home and explained everything to my fiancée. I decided that a move was now long overdue to ensure that I didn't end up, at best, not being able to look at myself in the mirror or, at worst, serving three years in prison as somebody's bitch.

CHAPTER 5

Holidays

Holidays had been a major part of my life outside of work over the last fifteen years or so as the household income increased and my credit rating improved, which gave me access to multiple no-interest credit card offers. I then used them to pay for the holidays, cleared only the minimum payment, and then settled the outstanding balance before the interest kicked in whilst, at the same time, putting the money into high-interest accounts and earning against the debt money. This was at the time of the new millennium, when the Icelandic banks in particular were offering savings accounts with huge interest rates. I can remember having six holidays in one year following this model of financial strategy: taking in New Year in San Francisco at the start of one year and Warsaw at the end of it, with visits to Las Vegas, the Maldives, Prague, and Dublin in between.

There were two other major factors in the shift in lifestyle at this time; one was the fact that our home was now fully refurbished to the point where both my fiancée and I were happy with it and no further major expenditure was required. The other factor was a major health scare for my fiancée that could have been so much more serious than it transpired but still established a shift in mentality regarding the work/

life balance that we had at that time. She had already admitted to me that she had taken a pregnancy test and it had been positive. This had stunned me, as it was definitely not a planned pregnancy.

A few days later, I received a call at work from my fiancée, telling me not to panic but that she had been rushed to hospital and requesting that I inform her manager. Once I had done as she asked, I then explained the situation to my manager and rushed off to my parents' house so that my mother could accompany me to the hospital, as I knew I would be too full of worry and concern to be able to process any information that my fiancée or the medical staff tried to relay to me.

It transpired that she had suffered an ectopic pregnancy, and luckily the emergency operation had been a complete success. When she returned from the operating theatre, both my mother and I were waiting in the room, the worry on our faces evident. She exclaimed, "Bloody hell, you two look far worse than I feel!" My relief at her being safe and in such good spirits was huge; the doctor had explained that it was possible that she could have died from complications brought on by the ectopic pregnancy. I am by no means a deeply religious person, but I have to admit that I actually prayed that my fiancée would be OK, which I realise sounds rather hypocritical of me. It was during her recovery that we decided that life was way too short, and having seen how easy it could possibly be taken away from you, it was time to see a bit of life outside the British Isles.

Whilst holidays became a way of rewarding ourselves for working as hard as we did, there was one occasion where I mixed a holiday with people I had worked with, which was certainly an experience and not one I have managed to repeat since and without doubt wouldn't be able to eclipse as a weekend away. I was working in the construction industry at the time, and Gary, my former colleague in public transport and my good friend, had invited me to a weekend in Prague that was being organised by his manager. Gary was now working in local government, having finally found an escape route from the boredom of that office, which was situated in a hell on earth. It was to be a long weekend, with apartments and flights booked for a dozen guys to experience the sights, sounds, and cheap alcohol of the capital of the Czech Republic. When the day to depart arrived, I was quickly introduced to everyone at check-in, as I only knew Gary, and we then decided to have our first drink at the bar to celebrate what we hoped would be an epic weekend.

On arrival in Prague, we organised ourselves into two taxis and headed to the apartments that were situated in the city centre. With our bags dropped and the beds selected, we headed out to sample our first taste of life and found a bar nearby that looked more like a canteen but served good strong beer for a fraction of the cost we were used to back in England. After a few hours, we headed to a restaurant that had been pre-booked in order to soak up the alcohol and allow us to partake in a little more. It was then suggested that a lap dancing bar was the obvious next location on our first night, although the rules are somewhat different to the establishments seen in Britain, particularly when it comes to what behaviour is and isn't acceptable with the girls inside. The first difference I noticed was the fact that we were ordered to hand over any cameras in our possession at the door; our reluctance to do so was not appreciated, and the doorman opened his jacket to reveal his revolver to us to suggest that it would be wise to do as they asked.

Inside, we grabbed drinks and tried to take in the atmosphere whilst attempting to look as if this was an everyday experience for us all. It didn't take too long before some of the girls came over to our table to introduce themselves to us. Admittedly, they were all attractive women, but I was happily engaged and simply not interested in a dance or any of the "extras" that were clearly on offer. Gary, having been through a hard time of things of late in his personal life, wasted no time in interacting with a beautiful black girl, his argument being that he could hit the town every night for twenty years and not hook up with someone as gorgeous as this girl, but for fifty pounds, she was his for an hour or so. Whilst I could completely see his logic, I knew I couldn't look myself in the mirror had I found myself tempted to cheat on my fiancée. My attitude was in the minority, but it was by no means a lone voice, as a couple of the other guys felt the same way.

Before long, it became obvious that Gary would be the first to head upstairs and experience the full range of what was being offered to him. In fact, we were all still sitting at the table when the fly of his denim jeans were undone and the girl was conducting some sort of abracadabra magic routine in trying to raise "Little Gary" from his slumber. Thankfully, Gary and the girl quickly moved upstairs, but we then had to hang around until he returned. When he did, it appeared that his fifty pounds had been a sound investment.

The first night ended with us drinking absinthe in a nightclub near our accommodation. Soon one of the guys began rubbing the absinthe into his thinning hair and setting it alight, much to the delight of the rest of us and the other revellers in the club (it probably comes as no surprise that the person in question was an amateur rugby player).

Having slept off the effects of the night before, we did what most groups of British lads on a foreign weekend away would do. We found a British pub where we could order ourselves a cooked breakfast and a beer (by the last morning, the beer had been replaced by mugs of tea in order to give our livers some respite). We then discussed what cultural delights we thought it would be best to indulge in on our first full day in Prague, such as the beauty of the St. Vitus Cathedral or the majestic Prague Castle. In the end, the landslide winner was a tour of the local bars to discover just how cheaply we could buy a beer (for the record, the winner was a quaint little ale house that appeared to be the domain of the local neo-Nazi chapter and who offered a decent beer for just fifty-seven pence).

By the evening, we were all, to a man, suffering the effects of our experiment – and none more so than Gary, who was finding basic tasks such as balance and walking in a straight line far more of a challenge than they should be for someone in his early thirties. On our way back to the apartment, Gary was accosted by two prostitutes who seemed keen to show him a good time but were actually relieving him of his wallet. A visit to the local police station the next morning proved fruitless for us and a number of other tourists who had also been robbed but by opportunist pickpockets that weren't dressed in high heels and miniskirts. The officers treated us as if we had defecated in their lunch.

On our final night, we again found ourselves in a lap dancing bar/brothel, but the ladies in this establishment seemed to be a little choosier about who they were prepared to do business with, as many of the girls that were approached by members of our group explained that they were "not working tonight". This made complete sense to me, as I would often spend my holidays sitting in my own office and wearing my best clothes.

As the night turned into morning, we found ourselves in Wenceslas Square, and Gary was keen to end his holiday "with a bang". When he found a prostitute he liked the look of and arranged a price and location (thirty pounds and the nearby subway station), I persuaded him to hand over to me everything of value he had, barring the agreed fee, to ensure that if he was be robbed again, he would lose only the money he expected to part with anyway.

He later emerged and explained that not only had he not been robbed, but that he had also received some rather pleasant oral sex in a photo booth in the subway station. Once I had established that he hadn't put the money into the booth to capture this romantic moment, he did admit to me that he thought it was the seediest thing he had ever done. "You *think* that's the seediest thing you've ever done? Do you mean to tell me that you're not fucking sure it is!" was my incredulous response. On the flight home Gary received possibly the weirdest compliment you could achieve from your manager when he declared that Gary had, without doubt, the biggest sexual appetite he had ever seen in a man.

One of my regrets throughout my many travels was not making more of an effort to speak the local dialect. Once a destination has been decided upon, I always begin with the best of intentions but never get much further than a rather poor schoolboy level of the language. I seem to be capable of generally understanding what is being said but lack the knowledge and confidence to respond in kind. This was never more obvious than on a trip to Central America and Cuba with my wife.

We had spent a week in Costa Rica and managed to get by with a few obvious Spanish phrases but were fortunate that most of the locals spoke reasonable English, no doubt as a result of the high volume of Americans that visit the country. We had taken a late flight back to Havana and now faced a four-hour journey to our beach resort in Varadero. We found our tour guide, who then negotiated a fare with a nearby taxi driver to drive us. Unfortunately, she selected one who spoke absolutely no English whatsoever. My wife suggested that on such a long journey in the middle of the night, we would probably be asleep in the back or could pretend to be to avoid the embarrassment of being perceived as typical Brits abroad who made no effort to converse in the language of the country we were in.

We had not been driving long, but sleep was already far from being an option for me, as the dusty roads we were travelling on were dimly lit and the car lights were providing images of scores of Cubans walking with traffic, hoping for someone to provide them with a ride.

My concern was heightened further when our driver pulled over without any sort of warning, got out of the car, and went to retrieve something from the boot. He returned with a bottle of water for himself, but I was far from convinced that this was his only motive, and no doubt fuelled from a mixture of tiredness, jet lag, and a total inability to communicate with this person, I became convinced that we would soon find ourselves robbed, murdered, and lying in a ditch somewhere. This fear then became heightened to ridiculous levels when we turned off the main road and travelled up a remote-looking track. At this point, I noticed that the driver had removed his tie and placed it next to his seat, and as I began to discreetly move it closer to me, my wife, who by now was probably in a state of mind to help the driver dispose of me if that was his plan, demanded to know what I was doing. I told her, "I'm keeping this close at hand, and if I get even the slightest inkling that he's driving us to our death, I will whip this around his neck and strangle the bastard!"

Whilst my wife was explaining that she would in fact murder me before I got the chance to garrotte our only possibility of reaching our beach resort, the driver stopped the car outside of a bar, where the owner explained in broken English that we could grab a drink and use the toilet facilities to break up our long journey.

In my early travelling days, it would take a while for me to loosen up and relax, as I would be uptight and on edge. I felt I had to carry the responsibility for the safety of us both and would carry a trust nobody attitude into our travels until I got to the stage where I felt it was safe. The biggest example of this was on our tour of Sri Lanka. The government had declared war on the Tamil Tigers and promised to rid them from the country completely just weeks after we had booked our holiday. Security was tight and apprehensive wherever we went, and our driver was stopped on numerous occasions but fortunately was always waved on quickly when it became apparent that his passengers were merely Western tourists.

As worrying as this was, I had little idea that a day at a spa in our first resort would have more frightening ramifications for me than anything that the resumption of Sri Lanka's civil war could throw at me. I had never been to a spa, and on my wife's recommendation, we booked for a whole day of therapies as a treat to ourselves and to fill a day that was expected to produce poor weather. We arrived after breakfast to be met by a huge man who was dressed a little like a doctor of some sort. He gave us a strange tonic to drink and then declared that I should go on a diet because I was rather overweight. Whilst this was undoubtedly true, it was more than a little rich coming from a man who clearly loved his food more than I did.

He then called two of his assistants and introduced them to us; one was a stunning-looking girl, and the other looked like a younger, larger version of the "doctor". Predictably, the young girl escorted my wife off to a treatment room while I dragged myself from my chair and followed my masseuse into another room. Once there, I was asked to remove my clothes, but what wasn't apparent was whether this meant *all* of my clothes. I took the opinion that I was over five thousand miles away from home and would never have to see this guy again so what the hell – I'd get completely naked. From what I could tell, this didn't seem to faze the masseuse, so I climbed on the table and prepared to be the most relaxed I had ever been.

The first treatment was an all-over body massage, but I found myself quickly wondering why it felt as if I were being put into a number of wrestling holds. My muscles felt as if they were being separated from my skeleton, and the masseuse was practising some sort of heavy metal guitar chords with my hamstrings and other ligaments.

After what felt like an hour but was barely fifteen minutes my torture was over (I was covered in bruises from this "treatment" a day later), and I was then ushered into a room that appeared to have an open casket in the corner, which turned out to be a steam machine with assorted leaves lying on it. I climbed aboard and lay on my back with my head sticking out the top like some naked magician's assistant while the masseuse closed the lid on my body. During the next fifteen minutes, he would pop his head around the door to check that I was not too hot, and before long it was time to climb off and be patted dry by the masseuse. It was then that I felt a strange sensation in the region of my bottom. I turned around quickly to see the masseuse smiling and holding up a leaf that he had helpfully removed from the crack of my arse, having lodged itself there during my steam treatment. Then, even more bizarrely, he presented the leaf to me as if it were a precious piece of memorabilia that I would cherish back home when my holiday ended. If this hadn't been humiliating enough for me, my next treatment ensured that I would be repressing the memory of this whole day for some time to come.

From the steam room I was shown into another treatment room that I noticed had a shower in the corner. I was about to be given an all-over body scrub but did not expect the description to be so accurate. I was barely minutes into this treatment and still so traumatised from the leaf incident that I was definitely not expecting to feel the masseuse's hand begin to gently positon my penis out of the way so that he could rub the body scrub into my testicles before continuing on to my legs to complete the task. When he had finished scrubbing, I was directed towards the shower so that I could remove the scrub from my body. Once I established that mercifully this was something the masseuse would not be assisting me with, I turned the water on as hot as I could bear and sat rocking back and forth on the floor of the shower, wishing the water could wash away my mental scars as well as the body scrub.

When I later told my wife the story of how my first spa experience had gone, she spent about forty-five minutes laughing uncontrollably before explaining that I should have had the common sense to ask for some disposable underwear. It took a number of years before I was brave enough to tell anyone else about my experience, and the person I confided in was my surrogate little sister, Tracey. After also laughing uncontrollably for about forty-five minutes, she then did what Tracey does best and asked me the questions that nobody else would think of: "What type of leaf was it?" and "How far in was the leaf?"

It took a great deal of determination to keep my annoyance in check before responding that it was a fairly normal-sized leaf, as my arse wasn't so big that it could accommodate something from a cheese plant or something similar. I added, "Exactly how far up my arse did you expect the leaf to have migrated given that whilst my bottom by no means resembles two boiled eggs in a handkerchief, it was also not the entrance to fucking Narnia!"

I sometimes wonder what the masseuse made of the events of that day. I imagine it being the poor bastard's first day on the job and here he was, presented with a half-white and half-pink fat and naked Englishman who couldn't tell when he had flora and fauna secreted in his orifices. I also imagine him recalling the horror to his wife or family and bemoaning their insistence on his taking the job in order to better his life.

CHAPTER 6

Redundancy

Having made the decision to get out of the construction industry, I was sure that another opportunity would present itself. I now had management experience and a proven ability to report to senior management. I just had to ensure that my desperation to get away from my current job came across as enthusiasm for any good roles that I was interviewed for, as well as be armed with some viable reasoning for seeking another opportunity after barely two years in my current role.

I was granted an interview with a company that operated within the airline industry, where I happened to be interviewed by a woman called Leanne, who was a former colleague of mine at my first employer. She and her manager, Audrey, conducted the interview, and it went very well. Leanne's prior experience of my abilities was an obvious advantage, and with the exception of my making a bit of a mess of an accounting question that was asked of me, I was confidant of securing a second interview. As it happened, they had seen enough of me to offer the role without needing to conduct another interview, so I accepted their offer immediately. I felt relief that my time in construction was almost complete, even though it was at the cost of fewer annual leave days and a 10 per cent pay cut. I saw this as a temporary issue that would resolve itself over time once I had begun to show Audrey and Leanne that I was the right candidate for the job.

I now had to break the news to Terry that I had accepted an offer to work elsewhere and would be leaving as soon as my month-long notice period was complete. He seemed a little disappointed but not totally surprised by this news. I then called Warren, the finance director at the head office, to have the same conversation with him. Warren was completely surprised by the news and sounded more disappointed than Terry had been. He asked if there was anything that he could say or do that would make me at least reconsider. When I confirmed that there wasn't, he was keen for me to book a trip down to the head office before the end of my notice period so that I could say goodbye to him and the guys on the team, with whom I had built up relationships during my time with the company. I got the distinct feeling that he perhaps also wanted me to explain in detail the exact reasons for my departure. If this proved to be correct, I would then have the dilemma of deciding exactly what my conscience would allow me to admit to, for despite Terry not backing me as expected over the Freddie incident, I was still torn between my loyalty to him and to Warren. I had managed to keep things on the right side of accountancy regulations and the law, but things were a little hazier from a moral perspective. Part of the reason I was leaving was that I could sense plans being made that wouldn't so much bend the rules as potentially smash them into pieces. The question I had to ask myself was whether I should relay my concerns to Warren so that he could perhaps intervene in some way or at least warn my replacement to be aware of such things.

The next morning while sitting at my desk, I could hear the familiar sound of Terry marching up the corridor towards my office. He stepped through the door, and I instantly sensed that he seemed to be in a different mood from normal, which became apparent when he explained the reason for his visit. He had spent the previous day successfully finding and hiring a replacement for me! It seemed that no sooner had I informed him that I was resigning and departed from his office than Terry began the search for his new finance manager. He explained that his reasoning for this was that he didn't want to risk there being a gap between my departure and my successor commencing the role, which seemed fair enough, but this wasn't his call to make. Although I reported to Terry, I also reported to Warren, who was ultimately my line manager, and I assumed he would be conducting a recruitment process similar to the one that he had when I took the role. As it was, Warren was having a new employee thrust upon him by someone who had a very different view on how he wanted a finance manager to perform. The new man, Harry, was currently carrying out a temporary role within the joint venture, but Terry had negotiated for him to be released by the end of the week to allow Harry to shadow me during the remainder of my notice period. Although I felt that Terry's actions rode roughshod to an extent over the effort and commitment I had shown him, I agreed to begin the handover with Harry the following Monday, partly because I didn't believe that Harry would be allowed to take the role given the circumstances in which Terry had selected him.

Not for the first time in construction, I realized that the right thing to do was not always the course that was chosen. It seemed a brief chat over the phone with both Terry and Harry was enough to convince Warren that the right candidate to replace me had been found, proving yet again that the faith I had placed in the senior management of this business acting appropriately was sorely misplaced. I was particularly disappointed with Warren, as I had a lot of respect for him up until that point and couldn't believe that he had relented and basically rolled over to allow Terry to get his way, particularly after having specifically stressed to me on several occasions at my interview to be vigilant and strong enough to stand up to any practices that I considered a little naughty. I was rather annoyed, to say the least, and couldn't shake the feeling of being somewhat unappreciated. So I decided that the best way forward was for me to hand over to Harry as professionally as possible and then use my visit to the head office to inform Warren of my exact reasons for wanting to leave the construction industry behind. What struck me most about that meeting was the blasé reaction I received from Warren regarding my concerns. On the flight home, I reflected that ultimately I had left with my conscience clear; the meeting had enforced the fact that my decision to move on was the correct one. This proved to be the case even more so when I discovered some years later that Terry had been made a director of the company.

Before switching employers, I had been asked to attend a day at my new office so that I could be introduced to both my team and the other members of the department as well as perform as much of a handover as possible with Frankie, the woman I would be replacing, as this was to be her last day. Frankie also drove me over to the airport to meet the team with whom I would be liaising on pretty much a day-to-day basis.

At the end of the day, and with as much handover as we could manage in the little time that we had, I was invited to Frankie's leaving party, which was being held in the flying club at the airport. This allowed me to begin building an off-duty relationship with my team as well as the twenty or so other members of the finance department. I also felt that it would give a good first impression of myself and help me to understand the office dynamics, as all thirty or so members of the department worked in the same open-plan office. The first thought that had struck me when I entered it was how cramped it seemed, so it felt logical to me that there would be occasions when we were not going to be one big happy family, particularly during the reporting cycle, when deadlines would be rather tight. I hoped that once everyone had had a drink, tongues would loosen and I would be allowed insight into who to be wary of and who to keep an eye on. To be fair, in the whole of the time that I worked there, I honestly do not recall too many occasions when tensions got that bad – and certainly not to the extent that I had initially anticipated given the three-to-one ratio of females to males that worked in the office. Without wishing to appear sexist or misogynistic, in my experience, offices with a higher ratio of females did tend to be less harmonious and wrought with arguments and rifts. There also seems to be a greater amount of bitchiness and backbiting than you find in a male-dominated office. However, this is purely my own opinion based on experiences in both male- and female-dominated offices, although I also have several female friends that prefer to work with men rather than women, as men seem to be thought of as being far less problematic.

Within about three months or so of joining the company, Audrey was replaced as finance director by a guy called Brian. He'd been carrying out some consulting work at the head office for about a month or so prior to this. (I've learned that this is a common way for businesses to operate regarding replacing senior staff; they employ an objective outsider to pry into how a particular director operates and then report on the findings. The director then either agrees to leave or is fired, but the smart ones tend to recognize the warning sign and ensure their destinies are in their own hands by arranging another position whilst under scrutiny from the consultant. Quite often, the consultant is then offered the role that has just been vacated.)

Brian introduced himself to the entire team and explained that changes may have to be made in the future to ensure the business could continue to operate as efficiently as possible. He also talked a little about his background, listing several companies that he had worked with that had either gone out of business or had ended up having to oversee severe staff cutbacks. It struck me that either Brian was incredibly unlucky or a complete jinx on any company unfortunate enough to allow him to set foot on their premises. It would not take long before it became clear that luck was most definitely not a factor in Brian's employment history.

The next day, I called a meeting with my team to see if anyone wanted to discuss Brian's announcement, as situations like this often tend to make people a little jittery. Some people can be quite averse to change and become concerned at what impact it may have on them. I assured the team that I would inform them of any further information on changes as soon as I knew and promised to take any concerns that they had to Leanne and Brian if necessary. Similarly to the construction industry, the profit margins within this industry tended to be very slender, and inevitably changes in the form of job losses were unfortunately rather common. Some businesses in the industry prided themselves on the quality of their product or service in order to justify higher prices to their customers, which can be perfectly acceptable if you are delivering those high standards day in and day out. For me, the business being owned by a venture capital firm was undoubtedly a major factor in the need for change, as their renowned reluctance to put their hands in their pockets for anything that wasn't a safety or legal requirement was well known.

Over the next few months, things appeared to settle down, and the changes that had been implemented to date were of no impact to staff numbers and of little impact in general to my team. I had gotten to know Brian a little better over this time and realised that he had quite a similar sense of humour to me. I remember being on an early morning flight with Brian and another colleague called Andy one cold day in November. We were heading to a conference at the head office for the day, and Andy looked nervous. He explained that he was not a particularly confident flyer, and he had the misfortune to be squeezed into an economy seat between my bulky frame on his left and the rather large physique of Brian on his right. As the aircraft taxied up the runway, I was doing my best to allay Andy's fears and assure him that the short flight would be over before he knew it. Just before take-off, the captain announced that he would be revving the engines due to the cold and that this was a perfectly normal practice and nothing to be concerned about. Brian exclaimed, "I fly three times a week, and I've never known that to be done before," completely shattering any confidence I had managed to instil in Andy over the previous ten minutes. I looked at Brian, and he was grinning mischievously.

About a month short of my anniversary in the role, I was called to a meeting with Leanne and Brian. I would be attending with my three closest colleagues, who were also management accountants but for other airports that we operated from and who also each had a team that they managed within the office. The four of us made our way to the boardroom to discover the reason for the meeting.

When we walked in, I noticed that the head of human resources was also present and that she looked terrible, in a bearer of bad news way rather than anything to do with her clothes, make-up, or general physical appearance. I suddenly got the feeling that I was about to be told some bad news, and unfortunately my instincts proved correct as Brian awkwardly opened the meeting and explained that he had been contemplating some changes in the office. Sadly, the major one involved all four of us being made redundant. The reason he gave was that at this time, none of us were actually fully qualified accountants and he felt that the business required personnel with this level of experience in order to help move the company forward. He explained he was happy to retain one of us as a junior to the three new recruits but that there would have to be an interview process if more than one of us was interested.

Once the initial shock of the announcement had settled within me, my first thought about Brian's offer of a junior role was one of anger and disgust. At no point had I any or of my colleagues (as far as I was aware) been addressed by Leanne or Brian about issues of work quality, inexperience, or poor performance, either formally or informally. Therefore, to have it presented to us as a reason for us to be relieved of our livelihoods was not sitting comfortably with me at all.

Leanne briefly left the room to make an announcement to the rest of the office and to let them go home early in order to allow the four of us to collect our things and leave without any awkward questions. This made sense, as my colleagues Holly, Mary, and Tiffany were all in floods of tears, whereas I, however, was far too angry to be upset, and I vowed there and then that I would prove Brian wrong and find myself a job with a company that appreciated what I could do. With the next day being a Friday, Brian suggested that the four of us should take the day off to allow this news to sink in and then have the weekend to get ourselves prepared to return to the office on the following Monday.

Back at our desks, I told the three girls that I did not intend to be absent from the office in the morning and that none of us had anything to be ashamed of so we should show this bastard that we were capable of being every bit the professionals he clearly felt we weren't. The three girls all agreed, so we met outside at nine the next morning and walked into the office together. We were greeted with hugs and condolences from everyone. Even Brian seemed impressed by our resolute attitude to his suggestion to effectively sit at home and feel sorry for ourselves, although I'm not sure he had felt that way five minutes earlier, when I had taken the opportunity for a little payback.

As I arrived at the office, Brian was unloading his briefcase from the back seat of his car. As he turned to walk towards reception, he saw my car coming into the car park and stopped but was clearly a little surprised to see that I was the driver. As I gestured for Brian to continue crossing the car park, I couldn't help forming a little grin on my face as he began walking and then suddenly stopped as his thought process likely registered that he was stepping out in front of a car belonging to someone he had made redundant less than twenty-four hours earlier. Having weighed it up in his mind, he seemed to add murder to the list of things he felt I was incapable of, and I somehow resisted the temptation of revving the engine as he quickly dashed to the safety of reception.

Over the next week or so, the four of us were individually called to meetings with Brian, Leanne, and human resources to discuss whether we were interested in the junior role that was to be created as well as provide us with details of other potential positions within the company that might be of interest to us. My anger at Brian's decision was still festering, and I spent a great deal of time preparing for my meeting. The wider business contained operations in locations all over the world, and a quick look on the internal website provided job descriptions of a number of accountancy roles in Europe, as well as both North and South America. I printed off the details to all of the jobs that I felt were within my levels of experience and pay grade and went armed with them to my meeting.

Whilst the emotion in the room was not at the same level as previously, it was still quite an awkward meeting. Everyone on the opposite side of the table from me was still clearly uncomfortable at what was about to be discussed. I was playing it cool. I was edgy inside, but only because I knew that I was about to make Brian look incredibly foolish if the meeting went the way I expected it to.

Brian asked what my interest might be in the junior role. "None whatsoever," I coldly replied. Brian then explained that there were very few other options open to me within the company and that none of them were accountancy related. "And what exactly are these options, Brian?" I asked. He then listed all two of them: an assistant planner role or one of the many minimum wage paying summer season positions that were required for peak travel times. These roles were mostly filled by university students in order to earn some money in between terms. "And they are the only possible roles available in the whole company at this time?" I asked. The question was so loaded that it almost burst before I could finish asking it. I then delivered the coup de grâce: "Because I seem to have found that these positions are available." I dropped the dozen or so job descriptions on the desk in front of the three of them.

Their embarrassment was all too evident; I had hoped to not have to play that card, but I had the overwhelming feeling that this management team were either unwilling or unable to put the interests of either me or my three colleagues first. Relieving people of their livelihoods is never an easy task to carry out, and in my opinion, the best way to deal with situations like this is to be as honest as you can and perform what is required with the level of professionalism and understanding that you would expect for yourself should the roles be reversed. From what I could tell, the image that Brian was portraying was one of "This whole situation is horrible, and I want it over with as quickly as possible so sod it – that will do," which had just added fuel to the fire as far as I was concerned.

After they apologised for not considering the roles I had presented and explaining that it was a result of not expecting any of the four of us to be contemplating working abroad, I was assured that they would look into the possibility of assisting me in any way possible in gaining interviews for these roles.

When I returned to the office, I told everyone what had happened and how I had made our esteemed finance director look uncaring at best and hopelessly inept at worst. I also explained that I may even get a few free trips abroad as part of any interviews. Given how foolish I had made Brian look, with hindsight I should have perhaps kept that opinion to myself, as it was inevitable that it would get back to Brian somehow. The help he had been genuine about offering to me at the time did not materialise, and I heard nothing from any of my applications. Had I not been too preoccupied about showing Brian in such a bad light to everyone and illustrating him as carrying out his duties so poorly, I may have been given the opportunity to gain at least an interview or two in foreign climes, which would have been a terrific experience.

I also took every opportunity to poke fun at Brian during this time, but it was never in a vindictive or personal way. One example was when he came to my desk to enquire about a report I was compiling for him. He noticed an accountancy magazine on my desk and read the headline aloud, which was "Inside, the Top 100 Finance Strategists". I couldn't resist the open door Brian had presented me with, and I went through it head first. "I didn't happen to see your name on that list, Brian. You must have been one hundred and first, I guess." To his credit, Brian flashed me a "You cheeky bastard" smile and walked off whilst I gave a mischievous wink to my colleagues.

Being an accountant, I had done numerous calculations to get a feel for how long my fiancée and I could survive without my having a job should worse come to worse. It amounted to roughly six months, which wasn't great but could have been much worse. As long as I could maintain some positivity about being offered a job again in that time, particularly during interviews, I was confident that we could keep the bailiffs from the door.

My three colleagues and I managed to strike a deal with Brian that meant we would be paid overtime for any additional hours we worked (as long as we didn't take the piss). We were also each promised a leaving bonus of a month's salary, provided that we left on a mutually agreed date that ensured Brian wasn't left in the lurch at critical times during the reporting cycle, especially as it was seemingly taken a while for him to begin the recruitment process for our replacements.

Within two months of being told that our services were no longer required, all four of us were successful in gaining employment. Unsurprisingly, Holly accepted the junior role that had been offered; I suspected that Brian wanted Holly for the role all along and should Mary, Tiff, or I have shown any interest in it, he would have ensured that it would be to no avail. The three of us agreed on the same leaving date from the company and were not only awarded a nice pen and a gracious leaving speech from Brian but also the leaving package as promised, with the added bonus being that it was paid to us at the pre-tax value.

For me personally, this was not only the best scenario in terms of gaining a payout whilst walking straight into a more lucrative position, but it was also a nice touch from Brian, as my short service meant I was entitled to very little in the way of redundancy compensation. It also meant that I had a sizeable start to the wedding budget I now required, for after a brief engagement of nearly eleven years, I would be marrying my fiancée in Las Vegas the following spring. In true accounting style, it was a decision made for all of the right reasons; chiefly that should anything happen to my fiancée whilst still employed by the police service, I would not be entitled to her pension unless I was her husband. And some people say that romance is dead.

CHAPTER 7

A Different Language

Over the years and in the majority of the jobs that I have carried out, I have had the pleasure, and sometimes displeasure, of dealing with colleagues, suppliers, and clients from beyond the shores of Great Britain. In my first job, I would regularly have to speak to colleagues from France, Spain, Germany, and Portugal, as I was responsible for clearing inter-company payments between our business and its sister companies in these countries. I was fortunate that their English was excellent, as my schoolboy French and German would possibly have allowed me to find the local post office but certainly not assisted in resolving any payment disputes that might arise. I didn't have any schoolboy Spanish and Portuguese to fall back on, so the fact that my counterparts had more than a grasp of my mother tongue was certainly a huge relief to me.

In those days, I had a rather strong regional accent, so I was concerned as to whether my European colleagues would be able to understand me. I had begun to develop a "telephone voice", as I had been speaking to customers and suppliers from across the UK as part of my grounding in all things finance, but I was concerned that this may not be enough to be understood internationally. This was in the days long before Google Translate, and email was still quite a new and exciting platform, so picking up the telephone and calling someone was still the main communication tool of the business. This meant that the usual British way of being understood (that is, shouting louder but still in English) was still an option, but any accompanying charades-like gesticulations would be a total waste of effort in this pre-Skype and pre-FaceTime era.

Overall, I don't recall ever having to overcome a major issue, thanks in no small part, again, to the level of English being spoken by my European colleagues. For my part, I made sure that I avoided slang words and colloquialisms so as not to confuse the issue or have to explain myself several times over like some idiot abroad. After a while, a rapport was struck with most of these colleagues, and confidence lead to us exchanging pleasantries and tales of what we had done over the weekend and so forth. However, this still brought about the odd "lost in translation" moment. I was once chatting with a German colleague and enquired as to what plans he had for the evening once he left the office. "I will go home," he responded. I asked where home was for him, expecting to follow this question up by requesting details of what his home town was like. "Home is where I live," he replied. My overconfidence at how well the conversation was going had led me to assume he would easily detect the nuance in my question and understand that it was a different way of asking the location of his residence rather than his feeling he had to define the English word "home" to an Englishman.

Dealing with people from other countries was a great insight into how they lived and operated in their work and in life in general. I also found that it embellished a few stereotypes about different nationalities. For example, any dealings I had with German colleagues or customers were always efficient and rarely incorrect, and they were always keen to establish that your request had been fulfilled to your satisfaction.

Another example is how casual and relaxed the people of the West Indies are in work as they are in life in general. When I worked in the airline industry, my team and I would regularly be chasing payment of unpaid cargo bills from the West Indies' national airline. They would always assure us that the payment would be made "soon" (this would often turn out to be weeks rather than days) and seemed perplexed at our anxiousness for payment to be made for bills "a little overdue" (often three months or more). I always found it difficult to be hard with them, as they were never anything but charming, and I envied their outlook on life more than just a little bit.

Many of the companies I have worked for have had parent or sister companies in the United States, and whilst I was never fortunate enough to visit in person, I have made some good acquaintances over the years through regular dealings on the telephone, or in some cases, they were lucky enough to have visited our sites in Britain. After a while, the main thing that struck me about dealing with Americans is their apparent inability to conclude a conversation, more so if it involves small talk rather than business. Once I noticed it, it would resonate and I would be unable to bring myself to help close the conversation, as if I got some sort of kick out of the awkward silence and the person then just drifting away from me, not knowing how to end our conversation.

This seemed to be something that also happened whenever a voicemail was left; I could always tell by the length of the message whether it was from an American colleague or not. The usual voicemail message from a colleague in my office would last about ten seconds and consist pretty much of "It's John Smith on extension one-two-three. Call me back when you get a chance. We need to speak about materials." Conversely, if the voicemail duration was anywhere between thirty seconds and two minutes, it was usually from a colleague in the States (apart from one occasion when some poor woman left an order for a Chinese takeaway one Friday evening). Generally, the American colleagues would want a similar request but would reiterate it two or three times in the same message and go into the minutiae of the query, meaning they basically had the conversation they wanted but without me at the other end answering their questions. The good thing was I could prepare everything before I returned the call, but for some bizarre reason they always seemed to talk through the whole query again when I eventually made contact.

In my experience, the generalisation that Americans do not get irony rang true on more than one occasion, one of which was during a visit to our plant by some finance colleagues from the American South who were conducting an internal audit of our business. One of the visitors was chatting to a colleague and good friend of mine called Chris, who was regaling him with the history of England. Suitably enraptured by Chris's knowledge of our history, the visitor announced his pleasure in the usual bombastic American way: "Wow, that stuff is always fascinating to me, particularly as we Americans don't have any real sort of history." To this, Chris replied, "That's right, because the Native Americans don't count, do they?" Our visitor smiled, and then again showing the inability to conclude a chat that was predominantly small talk, he slowly skulked away in silence but was, without doubt, completely unaware of the sarcasm and irony that was laced in Chris's response to him.

Without doubt, the most challenging and eye-opening foreign encounter I have experienced was whilst working for a manufacturer in the North of England who had a Middle Eastern customer. The plan was for some delegates to fly into London before catching the train north to our site, where, over the course of several days, they would be given a tour of the products they had ordered, we would discuss some minor contractual issues, and they would be entertained during the duration of their stay. What quickly became apparent was that the delegation was to number roughly a dozen rather than an anticipated two or three. It also became quite clear that all costs associated with the visit would be picked up by my company.

Ahead of their arrival, the rest of the project team and I were busy organising things such as a prayer room on the site (not easy, given it has to be an office of reasonable size and condition as well as facing towards Mecca) and ensuring that our staff canteen could deliver food and beverages that were suitable for the Muslim religion. Organising the catering would have been a challenge even for candidates on *The Apprentice* given that the canteen staff, whilst lovely people, were not exactly familiar with such things as halal meat. There was a form to be completed, and such items were never going to be found on it, especially as room for more new and inventive selections was occupied by options for port and cigars. This was a throwback to the good old days, when company directors could have extended lunches and then sleep them off in their offices before driving themselves home. We got there in the end, mainly thanks to the staff's ability to drive to a Marks & Spencer. However, we did have one or two oddities due to the canteen staff's inventiveness, such as slices of cucumber in a bowl of water, which is obviously a natural thing to do to a product that is 90 per cent water to begin with.

A team from our sister company had met the clients at Heathrow Airport and escorted them to King's Cross station for their train north, where my project team and I met them. My first impression was that most of the Middle Eastern delegates must have been struggling with a severe form of jet lag, as their balance was off and their speech was a little slurred. It had to be this because the only other explanation I could think of was that they had been boozing solidly since boarding the train, and I knew, due to a friend who is married to a Muslim, that alcohol is very much against their faith. We had arranged a luxurious minibus to whisk the delegates off to the hotel that was booked for them, one of the best in the city (we had been instructed to book the top two floors for the duration of the visit; the main guy was to occupy the top floor, with everyone else on the second floor). However, the plan went awry almost instantly, as the head delegate demanded to be taken straight to the site to inspect his merchandise.

Agreeing to this request, we arrived at the site and began to attempt, and subsequently fail, to persuade the delegates to adorn the required safety wear needed to access the manufacturing area. It was now obvious to me that the delegates' "jet lag" was actually the effects of indulging in the Western lifestyle more than their religion would find acceptable. I felt particularly sorry for our site manager, who was now trying to ensure that an ill-equipped, intoxicated, unsuitably attired head delegate didn't fall from a platform and injure either himself or someone else. Seemingly satisfied with what he had seen, the head delegate then demanded to be taken to his suite to freshen up before dinner. I had been invited to the meal and had been in two minds about attending, but given what I had seen so far, a business dinner with the potential for some unscheduled entertainment was far too tempting to reject.

The hotel had arranged a room where we could entertain the delegates and provide a meal and drinks. This was deemed acceptable, but the delegates appeared particularly keen to sample the local nightlife whilst they were in the region, so a few members of the team began to plot a route around the city in order to show our clients the best it had to offer. Unsurprisingly, a vast amount of alcohol was ordered to accompany the meal – and not just for consumption by our team. Towards the end of the dinner, I noticed that the head delegate appeared to be asleep in his chair, no doubt a result of the travelling and the nature of his refreshment throughout the day. Moments later, he woke up, banged his fist on the table, and demanded to know why he had not been taken to inspect his merchandise. I looked at the rest of my team, and we were all clearly confused and unsure as to how we should respond to this accusation without causing any offence.

Looking at the other delegates for help or even a hint of the best way to approach this situation proved futile, as they all sat with their heads bowed and wearing expressions that said, "I know we visited your facility this afternoon, but if he says he hasn't been shown the products, then he hasn't been shown the products." With nowhere else to go, our team leader did the only thing he could and apologised before promising to provide a full and detailed tour of the site and the clients' products the next day.

When dinner was finished, we boarded the minibus and set off to the first destination of the night, which was one of the city's best bars. It was quickly made clear that this was not the sort of entertainment that the delegation had in mind. Girls were the order of the day, girls who would happily remove their clothes for the delectation of their audience.

Once we arrived at was felt to be the best lap dancing bar in the city, I noticed our team leader handing his company credit card over to the bar staff and opening a tab for whatever was to unfold in the next few hours. I'd genuinely had no clue we would be going there, but fortunately a few members of our team were from other sites so they regularly stayed in the city through the week and thus had more than a little expertise in such matters. Drinking quietly in a corner with one or two of our team members, I noticed one of the delegates engaged in conversation with a lap dancer. This intrigued me because I couldn't remember this guy speaking at all up to this point, and certainly what he had said had not been in English. Inquisition got the better of me, so when their conversation ended, I went over to the girl to ask what he had said to her. She said that he'd told her to come to his hotel room now, adding that he had said the same sentence to her about fifteen times, clearly without success.

Thankfully, the rest of the night and the rest of the visit proved to be rather uneventful. The clients departed for London in good spirits (pardon the pun), and we were left feeling a mixture of relief and exhaustion. I would later add the feeling of sheer terror when the expenses for the whole visit began to appear.

CHAPTER 8

Separation

Sunday, September 12, is a day that will live long in the memory for me. It was the day that my wife, looking out of sorts, nervously played with her wedding ring whilst she explained that she had something to tell me but was reluctant to do so, as she knew it would break my heart. She then said the five words that did exactly that: "I don't love you anymore." I was still struggling to comprehend this when she then declared that she would pack some things in a bag and go stay at a friend's house for a few days.

This was all a huge shock to me, something I had not seen coming at all. It was not as if we had been constantly arguing for the past few months or finding ourselves with fewer things in common than before, which perhaps would have suggested that the writing was on the wall for our relationship. I was having a great deal of trouble formulating questions that should be obvious to ask by anyone who had been delivered such crushing news. Eventually, whilst she packed a bag, I was finally able to ask how long she had felt like this and whether there was anyone else involved. She replied that her feelings had built up over the past six months or so but that there was nobody else. She had just fallen out of love with me.

I felt like someone who had been placed in front of a firing squad and received numerous bullet wounds from the most unlikely source imaginable. As she made to leave, I begged her, actually fell to my knees and begged her, to take some time to consider what she was doing. She promised to give it some thought and, before leaving, proceeded to give me the most incredibly insipid hug. It was then that it truly struck me that my sixteen-year relationship with this woman was – at best – hanging by the tiniest of threads.

Still in a state of shock, I sent a message to my manager, Ed, explaining what had happened and that I thought it doubtful that I would be in the office in the morning. His reply suggested that he was just as shocked as I was about this, but he assured me not to worry and to concentrate on dealing with the things happening in my personal life. The truth was I had absolutely no idea how to deal with any of it; part of me was still clinging to the hope that she just needed a little space and time to herself, but I feared that things were far more serious than that. I also had the issue of deciding what to say to my parents. They were due to go on holiday within a week, and part of me didn't want them to cancel or for this bombshell to spoil their break, as they both worked very hard for what little time they got to enjoy themselves. I thought the best thing to do was to keep it to myself until they got back, as I would know more by then anyway and didn't really have a great deal of information at this point.

My plan lasted about eighteen hours. After one of the worst night's sleep imaginable, I was at the stage where I had to talk to someone about what had happened. I had found myself looking out of the bedroom window at every sound during the night, hoping that it was my wife returning, and then checking my phone for any missed calls or messages from her. When I spoke to my parents, they were as shocked as I was and could not understand where all this had come from. I sent a message to my surrogate little sister, Tracey, to let her know what had happened, and it took a lot of convincing that this wasn't a prank. She only accepted it when I urged her to go speak to Ed for confirmation. Again, she was another person who could not believe the story that was unfolding.

A few days later, I was at home, I was cleaning the oven as a way of keeping myself occupied when I heard a car pull up outside. It was my wife. She had arrived unannounced and wanted to talk to me. It was then that she confirmed that she had thought about things and decided that she would be leaving me and not returning. She also admitted that there was in fact somebody else involved and that he was a work colleague who was married with children and about fifteen years older than she was.

For the second time in the space of a few days, I sat in stunned silence, unable to comprehend what was coming out of the mouth of someone I had known and loved for half of my life. I somehow managed to ask how long the affair had been going on, and her response was about two months. She then expressed how sorry she was and that she would start to collect her things if that was OK with me.

At this point, I knew I couldn't remain in the house whilst she did this, so I made her promise me two things: that we would keep things as civil as possible and that I was to know nothing about the new man in her life. I was concerned that the latter would lead me towards a path that I did not want to tread for fear of being unable to control my emotions or behaviour. I then asked her to move her car so that I could leave, go to my parents, and let them know what had happened.

When I had the discussion with my parents, the three of us just sat there in total disbelief at what was occurring. None of us seemed capable of actually registering the events that were unfolding. I sent Ed and Tracey messages to let them know, and both were incredibly supportive. I also sent messages to a few key friends and family explaining what had happened, asking for some time to come to terms with things.

Later that week, Ed arranged to meet me for a drink in a bar that was halfway between the office and home. He wanted to check that I was still functioning as a human being and not disintegrating into a shambolic alcoholic mess. After giving me an enormous hug, he suggested that it might be beneficial for me to return to work the following week, and

I agreed. I requested that he pull the rest of the team together in the morning and explain to them the reason for my absence. My theory was that I could not guarantee my state of mind or emotions in the office until I was actually there, so if my colleagues broadly knew the story behind my absence, then they would also understand why I might be acting a little differently than usual. I also decided that it would help to talk about things with some of my colleagues who were not only good friends but who had also been through similar situations themselves. I knew that most people would want to know the full story but not everyone would be asking out of concern for me. Only those I knew truly cared about me would be getting the sordid details.

That Monday, I arrived early to ensure I was in the office before anyone else. This proved problematic, as the urge to get up and leave was enormous until people slowly started to arrive. My colleagues were stand-offish initially, almost seeming to want me to make them aware of my mood so that they could then act accordingly. Ed had insisted that as long as I was around people and occupying myself, he wasn't too concerned with what work I did.

Tracey had booked a meeting room, and the first chance I got, I went over to speak to her. We sat in the meeting room for most of the morning, and I told her the details of what had happened over the past week. She gave advice and talked about some of her own experiences. It must have looked decidedly odd to people passing by that we sat there side by side for so long without a computer and passing tissues to each other as we cried our eyes out.

Whilst I was still very much coming to terms with things, it seemed my wife had moved on emotionally and was now messaging me, asking me to make a decision on whether I was staying in the house or wanted her to buy me out. I explained that I was struggling with the coldness of her correspondence after so long and that as far as I knew, she hadn't told her parents or brothers about what had happened. I insisted that she do this before I made a decision. Inevitably, the fact that my wife hadn't informed her family was providing me with hope that this was all a bad experience and that everything would return to normal shortly. With hindsight, I cannot understand how I ever thought this way, as she was being very clear about our marriage being finished. I was blocking out valid thoughts regarding being unable to trust her again after betraying me so badly.

My insistence to my wife that she tell her family everything before I made a decision on the house was driven by a hugely uncomfortable and upsetting telephone call I had received days earlier from an uncle of hers who lived in France. He wanted my wife to assist him with some paperwork and was clearly unaware of what had recently happened. I spent the whole conversation acting as if everything were normal before sending her a message to let her know that he had called and needed her help. Many of my friends were amazed that I hadn't just told him exactly why she wasn't there and explained to him precisely what his niece had been up to, but I guess I was protecting her because I still cared for her despite what had happened. Besides, I didn't see what good taking that attitude would have done anyone.

About two weeks had passed, and I had arranged a meeting with my wife, for there were obviously a few questions that I desperately needed answers to regarding what had happened. Ed had advised me to draw up a list of questions to take with me so that nothing was overlooked due to the emotion of the occasion. This was sound advice, as it was best for all concerned that every outstanding issue was resolved in one hit, for it would not be healthy for either of us to drag things out over several meetings, as much as it would still have felt good at this point to see my wife and spend time with her.

I figured that the best venue for the meeting to take place would be a neutral one, so I chose the same beach location that we had driven to on our first date. It felt right to end our journey in the place it started all those years ago as young sixth-form students. I also hoped that the weather would be slightly more favourable than it was on that dull, grey Wednesday towards the end of March. I spent the days before our Saturday meeting ensuring that my list of questions contained everything

I would need an answer to. I had consulted with some family and friends in order to cover any potential gaps that I may have overlooked regarding collection of her remaining belongings and issues connected to my buying her out of the marital home.

On the Thursday before our meeting, I visited the doctor for the results of a check-up that had been carried out on me the week before; it felt right to explain the situation in my personal life to my doctor in order to gauge where I was with regards to my physical health. She performed a number of tests and advised me, unsurprisingly, that losing some weight would not be a bad idea given the fact that I was bordering on being morbidly obese for my height, as well as the fact that my arteries were sounding as tight and furry as Sooty's anus. There was also the fact that my father had been diagnosed with type 2 diabetes.

The result of one of the tests then inflicted another huge dagger in my heart as well as provided another question to add to my list, only this was one that I really did not expect to have to broach with my wife at our meeting. It seemed that the urine sample I had provided was showing the possibility of an infection that required further analysis, and the doctor advised that in the meantime, I should get in contact with any sexual partners that I may have had from the previous three months. My imagination immediately went into overdrive. There had only ever been my wife, so there was no danger of this being a long list. But it was dawning on me that it was quite possible I had not only lost my wife to another man but also that I may have potentially been handed a leaving present. And to top things off, I would now have an agonising wait to discover the severity of what I may or may not have contracted.

When the day arrived, I was at the beach a little early, mainly through my keenness to get on with it as well as to get the first question and its shocking and unsavoury nature out of the way as quickly as possible. I couldn't see my wife or her car, but she appeared within about five minutes and walked towards me. We found a quiet spot to sit down, and I dug out my list of questions. I could see that she was a little daunted by the length of the list, but I also sensed some relief in the fact that this should ensure that no follow-up sessions would be required because of omissions or forgetfulness.

When I broached the subject of potentially having contracted a sexually transmitted disease and that she may want to carry out a medical check-up of her own, her reaction was unexpected. She didn't appear as shocked or worried as I was about the situation – just much more hurtful. From my perspective, it become obvious that she had clearly not been very careful throughout her affair with her new man.

We spent the next couple of hours or so going through my remaining questions and her responses. We agreed to arrange a suitable date and time that would allow her to collect the last of her belongings from the house. I even offered to box everything up for her (at the time, some friends couldn't understand why I had not turned her remaining belongings into a burning pile of rubble on the front lawn, but I couldn't see the point or what I would gain from that other than perhaps five minutes of vengeful satisfaction).

Just before we concluded, I reminded her that the one thing I had always said to her was that I would always do anything for her and that if that now meant I had to let her go, then so be it. As we went our separate ways, she gave me what felt like, and turned out to be, a huge goodbye hug. We were both tearful, and I made her promise not to drive away until she had composed herself. She agreed on the condition that I promised her the same thing, to which I replied, "I don't think I have enough provisions in the car to last me until Monday." She smiled and told me that even after all this time and everything we had been through in recent weeks, I could still make her laugh. Then she was gone, becoming someone that I used to know rather than my wife, partner, and soul mate of over sixteen years.

As it happened, the additional test results came back negative. There was no infection for either of us, but at the time, it was certainly a worrying position for me to be in and further proof that my life was moving in a different direction quickly. I knew that I needed to try to gain control of it as fast as I could.

As the days and weeks passed, things gradually started to get a little easier for me, although from time to time, certain things like a song or a memory would still trigger me to seek sanctuary in the toilets at work or have a minor meltdown in the car on the commute either to or from the office. On the whole, I was improving and moving on from the initial shock of what had happened, albeit quite slowly, and beginning the process of rebuilding my heart from being a million-piece jigsaw puzzle that had been thrown to the floor.

Then one final hammer blow was delivered regarding the separation. I was sitting at home with my parents one evening when the telephone rang. When I answered, a female voice enquired as to whether I was the owner of the house, and before she actually introduced herself, I instinctively knew that I was speaking to the partner of the man who was having an affair with my wife. She explained that her husband wasn't providing her with any information and that she was looking for details regarding their affair to act as evidence for her upcoming divorce.

Somehow I remained calm, measured, and polite throughout the entire conversation as I explained to her that I could not help her and that it would be best if she left me alone and spoke to her husband instead. I then hung up and relayed the conversation to my parents, who initially had assumed that my wife's new lover was the one who had called. For the first time since my wife had walked out, I was angry. Again my imagination was running wild and firing questions in my head, such as how had this woman known my contact details? Did she have my address? Would I come home one day and find her camped on my front lawn with her two children in a desperate attempt for answers to questions that I quite probably wouldn't have been able to provide her with in any case? Also, how much of a spineless twat was this new bloke of my wife's that he hadn't explained the situation to his wife and teenage children as my wife had done with me?

I sent a message to my wife explaining what had happened and demanded that she hand over the only pair of testicles that clearly existed in her new relationship so that he could then go and inform his wife of what was going on. I explained that if I received one more phone call from this woman or she was to come to my home, then I could not guarantee that the level of reasonableness I had shown up to this point would continue.

My wife later informed me that she believed it must have been an unknown colleague of hers who had decided to pass my name, address, and telephone number to the wife of her lover due to their disgust at what they had done, supposedly in the hope that I would provide her with any information I may have due to the fact that she was receiving absolutely nothing from her own husband. I was still angry at the fact that my wife's new man could have ensured that this whole situation was avoided by doing the decent thing by his family in the first place and confessing to the affair and communicating what his plans were.

My wife apologised to me on his behalf, which did nothing to improve my mood. I was also somewhat angry with myself for still being protective of my wife by refusing to engage with this woman, even after all the hurt that I had suffered, the final irony being that this woman apparently thought I sounded like a decent man, despite the fact that I refused to help her in any way.

Over the next few weeks, I began jogging every morning. I was still having trouble sleeping, so it seemed logical to use what was becoming my natural wake-up time of five in the morning as an opportunity to pound the streets when it was dark. At such a time, there would be little chance of anybody seeing me huff and puff my way around the local housing estate. I was soon doing three miles every morning before work, and combined with my lack of appetite, I was losing considerable amounts of weight each week and becoming fitter and healthier by the day. My theory was that if I was ever to find someone new to share my life with in the future, I would stand a better chance this way.

Over time, I didn't seem to be able to take myself past the well-worn three-mile circuit that I had cut out for myself near my home. It was only when I spoke to a colleague in our southern office, who advised me that I only *thought* I couldn't run more than three miles, that I actually gave it a go. Three years on, I am now the proud owner of three half-marathon medals and have also raised hundreds of pounds of sponsorship for a charity that another colleague in the southern office had set up in memory of his son. It felt good that something so good could stem from such a heartbreaking situation and that I could help the lives of others whilst ensuring that my own health improved at the same time.

It's close to five years since this whole episode unfolded. I am on reasonable terms with my ex-wife, but we rarely communicate. The truth is that there is very little need to do so because the divorce has been finalised, the assets have been apportioned, and we live in different areas of the country. The chances of bumping into each other are incredibly remote. There was a time when I had hoped for some sort of relationship with my ex-wife because she was such a huge part of my life for so long. However, it has become obvious to me that things have progressed to such an extent that it seems better to leave things as they are and move on with my life as it is. I'm in a happy place right now, and I no longer see her as the glue that held me together, mainly due to the fact that I know I have others around me who are there for me and always will be.

CHAPTER 9

Working Away

Working away from home was something I was always generally comfortable with. On the plus side, it gave me the opportunity to travel to new places and meet new people. The downside was that at times it could be an inconvenience, particularly during my marriage, as it meant an unwelcome break from spending time with my wife, but once I was separated, I allowed it to become a huge part of my work role. It gave me the opportunity to think things through whilst travelling, and if I'm honest, it was often used as an excuse to avoid having to deal with issues that always arise following the breakdown of a marriage.

My employers must have seen me as somewhat of a godsend. Here was someone with no commitments who was willing to travel the length and breadth of the country (and abroad) at little notice to attend meetings or carry out internal audits of other sites. They could therefore avoid the usual issues of staff grumblings due to childcare problems or some employees' general reluctance to being away from the family home.

On one such occasion, it was early December and I was at my then-company's head office in the South of England. I was attending a workshop as a member of a team tasked with designing a new business risk tool that, if successful, would be rolled out across the whole of the

UK company operations. The team was headed up by a colleague of mine called Tim. After finishing for the week, Tim and I said our goodbyes to the rest of the team and made our way to the airport to catch our early evening flight back to the North.

On arriving at Heathrow, it soon became apparent that things were not running smoothly. The airport check-in area was like a scene from a refugee camp. Pandemonium was in front of us, and we needed to find out what impact this was inevitably going to have on our plans. We were informed that virtually all North European departures had been cancelled due to severe weather. It had been snowing heavily for several days, and temperatures were currently well below freezing. It was obvious that we weren't getting on a plane anytime in the near future.

Tim and I spent a few minutes trying to work out what our options were. We rang our manager to explain the situation: we had no flight and no car to drive ourselves back home, having just returned it to the rental company. The instruction was to find ourselves a hotel for the night and look to get booked on a flight home the next morning. However, sensing the chance of an all-expenses-paid night in London, we argued that trying to find two hotel rooms anywhere near the airport would be virtually impossible, not to mention ridiculously expensive, and there would no doubt be an almighty scramble for any available flights the next morning. So instead, we proposed that it would make more sense for us to make our way into the capital for the night and book ourselves on one of the many trains that would be heading north from King's Cross in the morning. We received approval to do exactly that, so we headed for the underground, excited at the thought of what this impromptu night in the capital might offer.

We managed to book into a hotel in Mayfair whose price was within the company's expenses policy; we were determined to enjoy ourselves given our circumstances, but we made the decision not to take the piss too much. We headed into Central London and found a restaurant near Piccadilly that served good steak. During our journey, Tim was trying to contact Eddie, an old friend of his who lived in London. Eddie worked in public relations and had treated Tim to some good nights out at restaurant launches and such as part of his job. The plan was to see what Eddie may have lined up for the evening and establish if it was possible that we could tag along and hopefully gatecrash it. Unfortunately for us, Eddie was instead heading out on a blind date, but we quickly persuaded him that if the initial meetup with the lucky lady went well that they should join us for dinner.

After a couple of pre-dinner drinks, Eddie and his blind date arrived at the restaurant; we sat down and ordered some food and drinks and got to know all about Hannah. It turned out that she vaguely knew Tim because they attended the same school, although she was a couple of years younger. After dinner, we decided to head out into the fleshpots of Soho and seek out some trendy bars full of cool people and even cooler cocktails.

In one bar, we bumped into Steve, a guy Eddie knew who also worked in public relations. Steve had just finished promoting the opening of a new lap dancing club in Leicester Square and was only too happy to put our name down on the door. Buoyed by the thought of free entry, free champagne, and ringside seats, we headed off. Fair play to Hannah: she didn't flinch at the prospect, and I remarked to Eddie that whilst that sort of attitude might suggest that she was not necessarily the type to take home to meet the parents, she may very well up ensuring that their first date culminated in a happy ending for him.

For the first and only time in my life, we breezed past the vast queue to enter the club. Our table was placed front and centre to give the best view in the house of the evening's "talent". The champagne duly arrived, and we continued the festivities. I must again point out that lap dances are not for me. The idea of a good-looking girl writhing naked in front of you and all the while you can't participate in any way seems the most ridiculous concept, bordering on masochistic, in my opinion. However, Tim seemed keen to see what all the fuss was about, whilst Eddie and Hannah decided to celebrate their blind date going well by enjoying a shared dance from a woman whose looks they both liked.

With the champagne drunk and the fascination over with, Eddie and Hannah waved us goodbye (as it turned out, to cap their night off in the style I had earlier predicted), so Tim and I hit the nearest club for a few more drinks and to soak up more of the London nightlife. By three in the morning, the club was closing. We spilled out onto the street, still eager to wring out every drop of our surprise night in the capital. Due to the sub-zero temperatures, the demand for taxis was off the scale, but there was no way we were going to waste what little drinking time we had left by standing in a queue for a cab, so we took the only sensible option available to us and flagged down a passing tuk-tuk.

Once aboard, our instructions to the driver, Dave (Tim argues to this day that his name was John; in actuality, it was probably neither), were to find us a drinking hole around Mayfair so that we could stagger back to our hotel with reasonable ease. Unfortunately, Dave/John either didn't understand our slurred instructions or was on commission from every lap dancing club between Leicester Square and Mayfair, as they were the only places he took us to. Pretty soon, our well-meant encouraging cries of "Faster, Dave [or John]", "Feel the burn", and "Max the envelope" were either not understood or, more likely, were totally pissing him off, as he quickly called our journey to an abrupt halt. He demanded his twenty-pound fee and left us to walk the remainder of the journey back to the hotel, feeling cold and still wanting that one more drink to finish off our crazy night.

Unfortunately, it was not to be. It was after four by the time we reached the hotel, and the night porter flatly refused to open the bar, despite the fact that we were residents. Defeated, we took ourselves off to bed for a few hours of sleep. The next morning, we checked out and dragged ourselves over to King's Cross. We managed to get seats on an early afternoon departure for a price that probably could have ended Third World hunger. The weather was still causing chaos, which meant that the journey lasted ninety minutes longer than normal, which felt like four days due to our lack of sleep and the mother of all hangovers.

Once the train pulled in, it was a brief but chilly fifteen-minute walk home for Tim. As for me, it was at this point that I remembered I had flown down to Heathrow earlier in the week and that I would now have to not only board another train to get me to the airport but also have to dig my car out of the three feet of snow that had fallen whilst I had been away. When I finally arrived home that night I fell straight into bed. It was Friday night, but I didn't care. I'd done enough revelling in my one unplanned night in London to see me through the whole of that weekend.

A more regular business outing around this time was the annual finance conference that my then-company held. This was an opportunity for the finance "family" from across the group to come together, learn how the business had performed over the previous year, and sit through numerous presentations and group exercises in an effort to "improve ourselves" as an accountancy department. For many, this was seen as the perfect opportunity to impress the hierarchy by appearing interested and asking pertinent, if not exactly challenging, questions of the senior finance executives. For others, it was the barely tolerable two-day means-to-an-end chore that allowed them to tuck into a free bar and capitalise on the unusually casual attitude the management took to the company expenses policy at such events. For the record, my own personal stance was somewhere between the two.

These conferences invariably took place in a central location to minimise travel for the majority of staff or near Heathrow Airport when we were partnered with the Scandinavian arm of the business. The evening between the two-day conference usually consisted of a meal, free drinks, and some form of entertainment. More often than not, the entertainment was a casino night, with the person gaining the most profit on his or her theoretical one-hundred-pound stake winning a bottle of champagne (as if to endorse the stereotype that all accountants are interested in is profit).

The mix of personalities, nationalities, and free drink always seemed to generate scenes that ranged from mayhem to the downright bizarre.

For instance, one colleague who had never stayed in a hotel before went to reception to complain that his room contained no light switches (it was a room where the key had to be placed in a slot on the wall to activate the lights), and the next morning he made the bed before checking out!

There was another occasion in the Midlands when an impromptu snowball fight took place in the hotel lobby; the bar was suddenly closed with no legitimate reason given as to why. To my knowledge, the company has not used that hotel since for such conferences. Whether that is through choice or not is another matter.

One year at the conference, I remember greed getting the better of me, which ultimately could have led to disciplinary action had I not apologised for my actions and been under the management of a very understanding boss in Ed. I found myself at a table of twelve for dinner for the evening; the company always made an effort to ensure that you were seated with colleagues from other business areas in an effort to promote networking, a bit like what occurs at a wedding, where members of both families don't just sit amongst themselves. The wine waiter came and asked the Scandinavian woman to my right whether she would be drinking red or white. She specified red and, against the odds, so did the following ten people before it was my turn to answer. With three bottles of cheap Pinot Grigio available, I could only give one possible answer: "I'll have white, please."

Unsurprisingly, I was still working my way through the wine by the time everyone else had left the table to mingle. I spotted a colleague and good friend of mine at an adjacent table. He had found himself in a similar position regarding the wine, so we pooled our Pinot resources together and continued for the next hour or so. Shamefully, I have few recollections of the remainder of the night apart from a drink spillage incident caused by the usual rush to order quadruple of whatever you were currently drinking before the free bar was shut down. I had my hands full of Guinness when Tim, my colleague from the unexpected London excursion, bumped into me in his own rush to be served before the clock struck midnight.

Now, a white top and spilt Guinness are not a great combination (unless you're looking to prove how great your washing powder is), but spilt Guinness on a white top that forms itself into the shape of a man's reproductive organs is something else altogether. My fresh new look was causing quite a stir at the bar and was probably proving to be a million times funnier to most people due to their state of inebriation. The stain had long dried and become less of a source of fun for the few people still around when I dragged myself off to bed some time later.

I used to have a quite astonishing body clock. For years, I had no need for an alarm, as I seemed to have a perfectly reliable inbuilt one that meant I never overslept. Even when I'd indulged in copious amounts of alcohol, it would never let me down. However, on this occasion, my body decided to hit the snooze button without my knowledge. I woke up with a start and looked at my phone; it was 8.49 a.m., and I had three missed calls from Ed, my manager. The second day of the conference was due to start at 9.00 a.m. sharp, and I had already slept through breakfast and most of the pre-conference refreshments. Somehow, through an immense hangover that was overridden by a combination of panic and adrenalin, I was showered and dressed in about nine minutes. My only hope was to get downstairs and hope that people were still grabbing coffee and slowly making their way into the conference room.

When I arrived outside the conference room, there was absolutely no one around; for the first and possibly only time in history, all 150-plus delegates were in their seats ahead of the scheduled start time. I looked at the seating chart to find out which table I was positioned at and scanned the names for someone, anyone, that I would have a vague chance of recognising in order to help me reach the table with the minimum amount of fuss and disruption. I was in luck. A former finance director of mine was at my table, so if I could quickly spot him and grab my seat, I could then pour myself a large glass of water before settling down to spend the first session of the day not drawing attention to myself. Instead, I could concentrate on sweating out a combination of Pinot Grigio and Guinness without being violently ill.

I entered the room and scanned it quickly for my table; I couldn't see the finance director anywhere. My presence had been noted, and a ripple of giggling started to fill the room as people's memories went back to what had now become known as my "Guinness cock" T-shirt. Due to what I can only put down as a mixture of panic and embarrassment, I franticly began to search the room for the table where I was due to sit. Each one was numbered (I was at number one, which turned out to be situated near the front of the room, which I put down to further karma for my behaviour the previous evening), but some helpful soul amongst the hotel staff had removed all the numbers from the tables. It was at this moment that things took a farcical turn for the worse. I was so busy looking around for my seat and trying to drown out the laughter from most of the room that I didn't notice a handbag on the floor in front of me. My foot went into one of the handles, and I began dragging it around the room, with its owner in hot pursuit of me. It was a visual comedy scene of which any of the world's greatest slapstick performers would have been proud.

Once free from the handbag and now in my seat, the laughter in the room finally subsided as the first speaker (a most senior director) came in to begin his presentation. My boss, Ed, was at a table behind me, and I heard a colleague mention to him, "That must make you so proud." The feeling of shame was keeping my headache and nausea at bay, but I know which I'd have preferred to have suffered, given the choice. The first chance I got, I pulled Ed to one side and apologised for any embarrassment that I had caused him. He was remarkably fine about it and was, if anything, relieved that I was OK given that he had struggled to contact me earlier in the day.

At this point, Ed's manager came over. He was someone I greatly admired (and still do). He was the man who had hired me when I had been made to feel worthless following my redundancy from the airline industry. He was also the man that I had been able to prove my worth to at a time when my professional confidence was at its lowest, so I felt the need to also apologise to him, as I would hate to have been the cause of any embarrassment to him either. Fortunately for me, he thought the incident was hilarious and commented, "The only way you could have topped that would have been to have come in still wearing your Guinness cock T-shirt from last night whilst carrying a pint, then put it down on the top guy's laptop before giving him a big bear hug and telling him that you loved him."

I spent most of the lunch break outside, desperately sucking in fresh air to ward off my hangover whilst regaling the whole story to my then-wife on the phone. She found it incredibly funny, but I'd learned my lesson and vowed to take a more sensible approach towards free drink on work outings in the future.

CHAPTER 10

From North to South

Around nine months after my wife walked out, I was working at my desk when my boss, Ed, came over and asked if I had a few minutes for a chat. We headed to an empty meeting room, and he came straight to the point. There was a need to fill a position in our office in the South due to an impending maternity leave, and he asked if I would be interested in the opportunity. I was then told that I had the evening to think about it but a final decision would be required in the morning. This role was to be treated as a secondment for me, meaning that the company would pay my travel expenses for the duration, which was anticipated to last approximately twelve months.

My initial reaction was one of uncertainty, but the advantages of taking the role soon became obvious to me. There had been a distinct downturn in business of late, and the future wasn't looking particularly bright at my current site. Job losses were beginning to look inevitable, so this could be a way out or, at the very least, a way of keeping the wolf from the door for a little longer. There was also the possibility of the person going on maternity leave falling in love with the prospect of becoming a full-time mother, meaning the position could become a permanent one. Not only would I be in the best position to take it, but

I would also have the advantage of spending a year getting to know if the role and the area were to my liking without it costing me the time, effort, and expense of formally relocating from one end of the country to the other.

I stayed in the meeting room and talked the offer over with my parents and some close friends. I even sent a message to my estranged wife for reasons that I believe were to test how she would react to such news. All it succeeded in doing was upsetting me to the point that I had to call Tracey from her desk to come down and rescue me from my latest meltdown. We headed outside for a chat, and I told her of the offer. I'd been sworn to secrecy, but I knew I could trust Tracey to say nothing. She offered me a hug, and as much as I felt I needed one, I knew that most of the office could see us and that many of our colleagues had a tendency to jump to conclusions. Moreover, Tracey was already becoming a target for office gossip, and I didn't want to make things worse for her, so I reluctantly declined her offer.

That night I went to bed with the intention of accepting the offer. Whenever possible, I prefer to sleep on decisions such as this to see if something changes in the morning, and if it doesn't, then that is the path I take. This decision turned out to be one of those cases.

With the offer accepted and the team in the South informed, it was then a case of booking some flights and hotels as soon as possible in order to spend as much time with Cheryl before her maternity leave began. It was agreed that I would catch the red-eye flight down each Monday, grab a hire car, and stay three nights in a hotel before heading back north on the late Thursday flight. Fridays would be spent in my current office. I wouldn't know too many people in the southern office, other than the finance guys, but I knew that Tracey visited the site most weeks for a few days, so I wouldn't be totally without friendly faces when I arrived.

Another element of the role would require me to spend approximately half of my time in the office of one of our customers, which was not only another new experience but also a chance to help improve relations between the two parties through not only my general bonhomie but also my baking skills, which were already proving rather popular across our sites and gaining some notoriety.

In the week before I began my secondment, Tracey challenged me to a bake-off. She chose macaroons, and we both brought our wares into the office. Our colleagues would eat one of each and select a favourite; the winner would be the baker whose macaroons proved the most popular. In fairness, neither of us had made macaroons before, and it certainly showed in the finished products. There was more than a little constructive criticism from the tasters ("They look like elephant dung" was a particular favourite opinion amongst the taste testers), but neither of us had any uneaten macaroons by the end, so clearly not all people eat with their eyes.

I raced into an early lead, which didn't go down well with Tracey; she is as fiercely competitive as I am, and I knew there was no way she would take this situation lying down. Sure enough, she became more selective about who she was asking to take part in the taste test, with good friends and known admirers of hers at the top of the list. Soon she had drawn level with me before actually pulling ahead, a fact she felt I needed to know instantly; therefore, she called me during a meeting I was in to tell me so.

I must admit that my competitiveness got the better of me and I allowed myself to react to her goading. I congratulated her on the fact that she was looking like the winner and had not done so in the manner that I had expected. I explained that I assumed that she would have come into the office dressed to kill in an effort to sway the vote, but to her credit, she had rocked up on the day looking quite dowdy instead. She slammed the phone down on me and called her then-boyfriend to rage at him about what I had just said; I put the phone down and reconvened my meeting to a room full of stunned faces who couldn't quite believe the conversation that they had just heard.

Later that evening, I received a Facebook friend request from an engineer who worked in the office. I knew him, but he was more of an acquaintance of mine and also a friend of Tracey's. Within minutes of my accepting the request, he posted a message that mocked the fact that I had lost the office bake-off; my response was lightning quick but measured: "Ben, I was never going to win over someone from the engineering community by delivering a quality product on time and within budget!" I'm still waiting for his response.

My first week in the South was long and tiring. The flight times were horrendous, and there was a lot to take in regarding the new role. Almost getting arrested due to a mistaken case of drunk driving wasn't exactly in my plans for my first week either. It happened on my second night. My hotel was centrally located and, as such, had limited parking. I'd arrived back late from the office and found myself unable to park my hire car, as there was a function taking place that night for either former rugby players or boxers (an assumption I made based on the vast number of flat noses and cauliflower ears in the lobby). I parked in the nearest public car park but noticed when I purchased the ticket that my stay was limited to four hours, meaning that I would have to move the car later that night back into the (hopefully quieter) hotel car park. Having had dinner and with my ticket almost expired, I went to retrieve the car. It was now quite late, so I was hopeful that parking spaces would be plentiful.

Unfortunately, a combination of the darkness, my lack of knowledge of the surrounding area, and a poor sense of direction found me heading away from the hotel and almost back to the motorway out of town. I somehow managed to get my bearings and headed back towards the hotel. It was then that I noticed a police van was following me. I checked my speed and deliberately allowed the driver a chance to overtake me, but that didn't happen. Instead, the driver flashed his lights and signalled for me to pull over.

Completely oblivious to any wrongdoing and by this time rather tired and irrational, I was perhaps not at my most friendly and accommodating when the officer approached. It transpired that the reason I had attracted attention was my slow driving and lack of any headlights! I had assumed the hire car had automatic headlights because it was similar to my own car; therefore, I hadn't bothered to check to see if they were active. Also, the dashboard was well lit, so I had not detected the problem. I explained this and also suggested that my slow driving was caused by the fact that I was new to the area. Fortunately for me, the other police officer in the vehicle was from a town not far from where I lived back in the North and recognised my accent. She explained that I would still be breathalysed, which, as I knew it would, returned a negative result. They sent me on my way, and I finally parked up in the hotel car park for the night. The story proved a good way to break the ice with some of my colleagues in the office the following morning.

My baking skills were instantly appreciated in my new office, once I had confirmed that they would make it safely through airport security and not be confiscated or lead me to be escorted away in an orange jumpsuit. My carrot cakes were a particular favourite amongst the team, with a few people wanting the recipe and various positive comments that ranged from politely kind ("the best I've ever tasted") to the repulsively kind ("My fingers are stickier than a teenage boy's on prom night"). Baking was something I really enjoyed doing. It helped me to relax and process things in my mind. It also made me challenge myself. Over time, I would take requests from colleagues to provide for their birthdays or if they were leaving the business. This helped me become part of the team quickly. My ability to work hard and be a team player would become apparent in time but didn't deliver that initial acceptance that the free cakes did.

My willingness to socialise outside the office was also a good way to build relationships with the team. In my second week, a member of our commercial team was having a few drinks in town to celebrate his departure from the company, and I had been invited. In the first bar, we were seated at a large table. People were chatting in twos and threes. Tracey was there and was attracting a few suggestive comments, as she always did. For some reason, some of the guys were messing around with the salt shaker on the table, and before long Tracey had accidently been covered in the stuff. My immediate advice to her was to "take it as a condiment", which she didn't find helpful but seemed to send the rest of the group into hysterics.

Near the end of the night, the few of us that remained were sitting outside a trendy bar, and we struck up a conversation with a couple of student girls. Talk was moving towards the next destination, with a nearby lap dancing club being favoured, particularly by Frank, whose leaving party this was. I was reluctant to go but eventually conceded given it was Frank's night and it was what he wanted to do. I'm aware that this is by no means the first occasion in this book that I have outlined spending a night in such an establishment, despite my protestations that they don't interest me (they honestly don't!).

I wasn't too surprised to hear that Tracey was happy to go, but it was more of a surprise that the two girls we had just met were keen on attending too. After paying our way in and grabbing drinks, a couple of the girls tried their best sales techniques on me, but as usual, I was not interested. In such situations, there is always an undertone of anything from frostiness to downright rudeness at this point, as the girls feel they have wasted their time and potentially missed out on another punter who perhaps was inclined to tip big. This being a quiet, nondescript Wednesday night in the South of England, I would argue that the girls would have to be incredibly unlucky to find a high roller walking through the door that night who was willing to lavish them with cash whilst they were busy wasting their time and efforts on me.

Before long, most of the group had ventured off to sample the entertainment, and I found myself talking to Jessica, one of the two girls we had met in the previous bar. I wasn't really trying my best chat-up lines, mainly because I have absolutely no chat-up lines whatsoever. After a bit of small talk, Jessica mentioned that she really liked the hat that one of the dancers was wearing. Feeling rather chivalrous, I told Jessica that if she liked the look of the hat so much, then I would go over and ask to borrow it so she could try it on.

Fuelled by chivalry and a sizeable amount of alcohol, I bounded over to the girl and asked to borrow the hat. "Twenty quid," she said. "What?"

I replied. "The hat is a part of me, and I cost twenty quid," she said. "But I'm not interested in you, sweetheart. I'm only interested in the hat." This response probably wouldn't go down too well with any woman, let alone one who uses her looks to boost her livelihood. With hindsight, I don't know how she refrained from slapping me for such a comment, and my next statement didn't exactly improve the situation: "Well, I'll wait until your back is turned and then just steal the hat." Her response to this was, as you can imagine, calm and measured: "If you come anywhere near me, I will call security and you will be leaving this place through the front door head first, you wanker!" This statement not only helped me to see reason but also seemed to sober me up instantly. Realising that my battle was lost, I trudged back towards Jessica, defeated and having to break the news that I had been unable to secure the hat.

Within minutes, Jessica made her excuses and went to find her friend. I last saw her locking lips with a guy called Simon from our office, who was, to be fair, younger, better-looking, and to add insult to injury, had actually worn the hat in question when he had received a lap dance from the same dancer.

Whilst I was enjoying my time in the South, an opportunity arose to take a job with another company back in the North; they were a manufacturing company that was relatively new but had signed a large contract to provide their services to a customer in the South Pacific. The role sounded tempting to me and appeared to be similar to a role I had carried out some ten years earlier. I had two interviews, and the view from the recruitment agent was that I had been so impressive that it was only a matter of time before a formal offer would be made to me. There was, however, one rather large stumbling block: the company were currently hiring office space at another business park away from their main site, and it was this team that I would be a part of, the issue being that this location happened to be in the same building where my estranged wife and her new man worked. Realising that the situation was now becoming serious, I spoke to Ed and explained the situation. Initially, he was disappointed that things had gotten as far as they had before I confided in him. I explained that things had moved very quickly from what was an initial look in the shop window, but I understood Ed's point of view. I told Ed that the deciding factor would be the working location, as my gut feeling was that it would be far from a healthy proposition to be in such close proximity to my estranged wife.

I sought the advice of family and friends and also sent a message to my wife to see what her thoughts were on the matter. No one thought it would be a good idea, which confirmed my initial instincts. My wife said that whilst she didn't have a problem with my working so close, she was unsure that it was such a good idea from my perspective.

With the decision made, I contacted the recruiter so she could advise the company that I no longer wished to be considered for the position. It quickly became obvious that if the company were looking at anyone else for the role, they weren't doing so through this recruiter. She pleaded with me to take longer to think about it and promised to talk to the company to see if the situation could be changed in some way, such as my being allowed to work special hours that would lessen the possibility of accidently bumping into my estranged wife. Whilst I'm not naive enough to think that recruiters always have your best interests at heart (in my experience, they are, on the whole, classless sharks when it comes to their responsibilities, especially with the smell of a deal in their nostrils), this particular crass response had me struggling to keep my composure. "Listen, take your commission hat off for just one minute, pretend that you have a heart, and try your best to understand the unique situation I find myself in here. Can you not see the issue I have and the potential harm it could do to me should I accept this role and find I'm not mentally prepared for the possibilities regarding witnessing my wife and her new man?" The recruiter went quiet and, admitting defeat, promised to contact the company and inform them of my wishes. It looked as if the South would be my home for a little while longer.

After several weeks, the early and late flights and the hotel lifestyle had begun to wear very thin. I was becoming resentful at the constant slog of being away through the week and seemed to be spending the majority of my weekend washing and ironing clothes, generally preparing to begin the routine all over again. The thought of this being my life for the best part of a year drove me to decide that it would probably be better to look for an apartment in the area. The company would pay for the rental and other associated costs, and it would prove to be a more economical way forward for them than the current arrangement.

I looked at a few properties in a number of areas and finally decided on an apartment in the city centre. I had to sacrifice a few things such as a parking space and a second bedroom, but it was by far the best place on the market within the budget I had. Having loaded my car one Sunday with as many possessions as I could, I drove south to begin my new life as a resident. The apartment was furnished, so the car was mainly carrying clothes and the odd creature comfort like a TV and DVD player.

I quickly settled in and worked out a jogging route for myself along the nearby harbour. To supplement this and to keep myself busy whilst I had relatively few friends in the city, I also joined a gym so that my weekends were occupied to an extent as well.

The lack of a second bedroom wasn't an issue until friends and family came to visit; it was an inconvenience more than anything else, but we made sure that it didn't stop us from having a good time. My parents would regularly make the long trip down to see me. Their visits were barely twenty-four hours long due to their work commitments and the duration of the journey, but it was always good to have them around. Moreover, I know it made them feel better to see me and know I was happy and healthy.

On a couple of occasions, my uncle and his family travelled over from London for the weekend to see me and to enjoy a mini break in the city. They always rented an apartment nearby, as it would have been impossible to squeeze them and my parents into a one-bedroom apartment with me.

Early one Sunday, I set off to the gym for an hour; my plan was to have a workout, grab a shower, and head back in time to spend some time with the family before they started to head back home. I dressed for the gym and set off on the walk through the city. When I finished my workout, it occurred to me that my bag didn't contain a towel for the shower, so I decided to throw my sweatpants on over my gym gear and head back home.

The harbour was busy on my walk back to my apartment. The weather was nice, and people were making the most of it. I seemed to be attracting some strange looks, but I put that down to not being dressed to impress. When I arrived at the apartment and walked into the front room, my dad took one look at me and said, "What the hell have you done?" I followed his eyeline down to the crotch of my light grey sweatpants, where I discovered a huge damp stain! My cotton sweatpants had absorbed the sweat from my gym shorts and given me the look of a man with significant incontinence issues. All those people staring at me on the walk back from the gym suddenly made sense. As a result, I now check my gym bag about fifteen times for a towel before I even consider leaving the house.

CHAPTER 11

An African Adventure

Whilst I have already covered working away in a previous chapter, one such experience stands above all the others, which I feel justifies having its own chapter. I was working in the South and had been quite heavily involved in an internal audit scheme for some time, having been trained to visit other company sites and conduct tests to ensure that their financial controls were at the required standards.

At this point, my trips had been solely in and around locations within the United Kingdom, with the exception of a visit to one of our Scandinavian sites. This was an experience I really enjoyed, although the cost of living for the duration was mind-boggling. Fortunately, the company was picking up all expenses. The trip took place in early summer, so the travelling and weather conditions were pleasant. Daylight remained until well into the night, and our hosts were welcoming and generous overall.

The few downsides included the condition of the hotel rooms, the theme of which appeared to be based upon that of a 1970s tower block in Czechoslovakia (in all fairness, the hotel was under renovation, but its pricing policy was still in line with that of most respectable hotel rooms in London). Another downside was the presence of one of our senior finance executives on the trip. My own personal relationship with him was always cordial, but he was the stereotypical accountant, with little or no people skills and an embarrassing habit of attending meals in the hotel wearing a pair of slippers that were so old and tired they looked like the favourite chew toy of his pet dog.

Eighteen months on from this experience, the possibility of having to audit the South Africa branch of the company came about due to discussions at the head office regarding a trade-off in which we would conduct this audit on behalf of the American arm of the business. In exchange, they would return the favour by doing the same at a small business unit that was located in the Southern United States and was under our control. The argument was that it would be more cost effective to do it this way, and there were enough degrees of separation between the two US businesses to not compromise the testing and risk a situation of "marking one's own homework".

Once agreed, there was then the matter of selecting the three candidates who would travel to South Africa to carry out the testing. I knew I had a good chance due to being on good terms with the organisers as well as being in the position of having no family commitments to negotiate. The only snag I could see was the timing of the trip; it was scheduled to be just ten days after my return from holiday in Fiji and could cause a great deal of disruption to my usual work commitments.

I have no qualms in admitting that I was desperate to go; this opportunity would not come round very often, and I knew that the organisers wanted me to go. I had proven myself hard working and reliable, and the flexibility that my personal life offered was an added bonus. I set about creating a plan of work that would convince my boss that I could either complete my duties or have a suitable contingency plan in place to ensure that there was no slipping of standards whilst I was in South Africa.

Suitably impressed, my boss gave the go-ahead, and I was confirmed in the party with a gentleman called Aled, from our site in Wales, and Olive, a good friend of mine from my time in our office in the North.

This would make the trip even more exciting, as we had always gotten on really well and had worked on the Scandinavian audit the year before. As the trip was to last two weeks, Olive also came up with the fabulous idea of organising a safari for the three of us during the weekend in between. We all agreed, and Olive, being the ultra-organiser that she is, sourced the best trip and booked it for us.

On my first day back from my trip to Fiji, I arrived at the office at stupid o'clock due to the jet lag kicking in. For once, I didn't mind this, for I knew I had a lot of work to get through over the next ten days and was keen to make a start. It was a long, hard slog to get everything complete or in place before I left on the Friday before the two-week journey to Johannesburg, but I managed to achieve it.

I then spent the weekend packing and preparing for the trip. We were flying overnight into Johannesburg and would be collected at the airport on Monday morning before being driven straight to the site, where we could shower and freshen up before beginning our work. Because of this and the length of the flight, the company booked us first-class seats on a Virgin flight. This meant that Aled and I would be chauffeur driven from our doorstep along the motorway directly to the airport terminal, whereas Olive would be flying in from the North.

When the chauffeur arrived, I was a little surprised not to find Aled already in the car. It turned out that we were afforded individual limos! For me, this was merely adding further fantasy to what was going to be an incredible experience. As you may be aware, when you arrive at the airport, you are driven directly to the terminal, where you are greeted by the check-in staff, presented with your boarding pass, and directed to the private security point and then on to the first-class lounge. Once there, I spotted both Olive and Aled indulging in cocktails and some snacks. I quickly joined them and ordered myself a drink. After quickly catching up, they both went off to get massages (purely because you could). I checked my messages and made a mental note to try not to shove this opulence down the throat of my friends and family too much …

When we boarded, we found our seats and settled in for take-off with glasses of champagne whilst trying to absorb the surroundings, and I struggled to comprehend the amount of legroom and facilities we had been afforded. Once the seat belt sign had been turned off, I went over and sat with Olive for a proper catch-up. We had not spoken for a while, and I hadn't had the chance to talk through the separation from my wife and the ensuing ramifications.

The flight attendant pointed out that the evening meal was about to be served, and I was about to leave for my own seat when she suggested that we extend Olive's table and dine together, which we did.

With dinner over, Aled and most of the other passengers converted their seats into beds and put their heads down for some sleep. Olive and I were still chatting, and we decided to sample the delight of sitting at a bar at cruising altitude. After a while, only the barman, Olive, and I remained. A flight attendant soon interrupted, abruptly informing us that people were trying to sleep so we should keep the noise down. Like a couple of chided schoolchildren, we skulked off to our beds to get some rest before our African adventure began.

After arriving and collecting our luggage, we made our way through departures and met our driver, Bruce, who was to be our personal taxi for the next fortnight. The drive to the site wasn't too long, and we took the opportunity to take in the sights and sounds whilst trying to adjust to the climate. Olive had been to South Africa years before to do some teaching and was reminiscing as things caught her eye on the journey.

Otis, the finance director, greeted us at the site. He was a large imposing man, but he carried a warm smile and welcoming nature. I briefly wondered if, depending on the results, that would be the case in two weeks' time. We quickly freshened up and sat down with Otis and his team to do introductions and explain the plan for the testing. Otis's secretary has arranged our hotel, and Bruce would be on hand to drive us to and from the site each day.

The first day wasn't particularly productive, mainly due to a mix of jet lag and gaining an understanding of the business and its systems.

The hotel we had been assigned wasn't far from the airport and so was a little out of the way; this was immaterial, however, as we were under strict instructions to not leave the hotel other than when Bruce came to collect us. Once inside, we saw that the hotel was a little dated, but the rooms were clean and acceptable.

I had just started to unpack and get some clothes together for dinner that evening when a horrendous noise broke out. I ran to the window and spotted a plane overhead that was about to land at the airport. None of us had realised just how close the hotel actually was to the runway until now!

We had agreed to meet in the bar before dinner for a drink and a look at the swimming pool area in order to get a feel of the amenities on offer. Olive noticed a black film around the edge of the surface of the pool water, but other than that and the extreme noise from the airplane traffic, the hotel seemed OK, although nothing special. Despite none of us being the type of people to be too fussy about food, we did struggle to find anything exciting on the menu. We all seemed to be thinking the same thing: *This menu is going to get boring rather quickly.*

After a somewhat disturbed night's sleep, due in no small part to the single-glazed windows being unable to counter the noise of jet engines grazing the hotel roof, we were driven to the site. During the course of the testing, we were discussing our hotel with some of the office staff. It was immediately obvious that they were somewhat perplexed as to why we had been booked into this particular hotel when there was a far better option in a different location. It had more choice of food and entertainment and the added bonus of being nowhere near the main flight path of one of the country's busiest airports. In addition to this, they also informed us that our hotel's best feature, the marble lobby, was a result of the hotel being held at gunpoint in the recent past, and it had been installed to help erase the memory of such an incident. They then went on and explained to us that the black film around the swimming pool was caused by pilots ditching aviation fuel whilst coming in to land in order to minimise the chance of the plane catching fire should a problem occur on landing! Convinced that we were not the victims of an in-joke amongst the locals, we decided to organise an evening at this other resort soon to check it out. If it remotely resembled the description we had been given, we would lobby our head office for a move across town.

We decided to spend Friday evening at the new resort as a nice way to start the weekend, but in the meantime, we were three nights into what was now known as the Runway Hotel and the dinner menu had indeed become rather tiresome. Therefore, we decided that the all-you-can-eat buffet restaurant across from the hotel could perhaps offer a refreshing alternative, and it was close enough to ensure that no real harm could come to us by wandering over for a bite to eat. On Thursday night, we did just that, and whilst the food was not a huge improvement on the dining room of the hotel, there were many more items from which to choose. It was also a chance to mix with locals rather than other business types or commuters who had missed flight connections.

The site closed early on Friday, so we had the afternoon to ourselves. It was another glorious day, so once again ignoring the security brief given to us back in the UK, we decided to change out of our office attire and take a walk to a nearby market and shopping mall. We were keen to procure some keepsakes for our loved ones as well as stock up on some essentials for our safari trip the next day. We took some photos of the local stores and of the Christmas tree in the shopping mall (it was mid to late November); it felt weird seeing decorations whilst walking around in summer wear, but it just added to the quirkiness of the entire experience.

That evening, we asked the staff of our current hotel to request a taxi to take us to see the other resort (another thing on the security team's "do not" list). The difference between the two resorts was incredible; they were polar opposites in everything from the hotel to the restaurant options to the casino and shopping outlets. This resort would not have looked out of place in Las Vegas, whereas our current residence was looking more like a battered old camping tent. It took no time at all for us to reach the conclusion that this was where we wanted to spend the rest of the trip. It also had free Wi-Fi, which would help with writing up the reports and allow us to maintain better contact with our home offices and our friends and families. We checked on availability and prices with reception and then contacted the head office to explain the situation and plead our case. They agreed, so we confirmed our check-in for Sunday due to our all-day safari trip on Saturday. Having had dinner and a look around, we contacted the taxi driver to return us to the Runway Hotel. En route, we mentioned to him that we would be transferring to this resort on Sunday and asked for a good price to do this. Unfortunately, his vehicle wasn't big enough for three passengers and all of our belongings, but he had a brother who could accommodate our needs, so we made a note of his telephone number and organised it for Sunday morning.

The next day was our safari adventure, and we were collected from our hotel and taken to a meeting point in downtown Johannesburg, where we would be transferred on to our coach before heading off in the direction of Sun City. A stop off about halfway allowed passengers to stretch their legs, use the facilities, and buy some souvenirs from various shops and market stalls.

The first thing we did was take pictures of ourselves standing next to another Christmas tree in forty-degree sunshine before having a look around the market for unique items to take home to remind us of our trip. Olive found a large giraffe that had been sculpted out of wood. She was very keen but didn't want to do the haggling that was commonplace in markets such as this, so I offered to do it on her behalf and threw in a much smaller version of the giraffe for myself in an effort to gain a better deal. With a suitable price agreed, we shook hands and exchanged rand for giraffes (now known as Ged and Ged Junior) and headed back to the coach. On arriving at our destination, we were given lunch and advised that we had about two hours free to use the pool and relax before our twilight safari would begin.

The safari was an absolute joy and, without doubt, one of the greatest things I've ever been fortunate enough to experience in my life. We were fortunate to see a pride of lions as well as rhinoceroses, hippopotamuses, giraffes, elephants, and a whole array of other animals and birds. It was an experience that we all enjoyed immensely, and I would not hesitate to recommend it to anyone.

It was quite late by the time we returned to the hotel, so we grabbed a light dinner and some drinks before retiring for the last time, excited at the prospect of transferring to paradise the next day.

After settling our hotel bills and checking out, we stood outside in the morning sunshine and awaited our taxi; it duly arrived, and we set off for our fabulous new resort. The friendly driver was informing us as he drove that he had never encountered snow in his life. At this point, I noticed that we were turning off the main road that we had travelled along on our previous taxi ride. We had ventured outside of our previous hotel on foot on two occasions, booked a taxi across town and back one evening, and now found ourselves in another taxi that was a recommendation of our previous driver (all situations that our security brief had forbidden us from carrying out before the trip). However, this taking a different route and being assured it was a shortcut left me feeling that we had perhaps pushed our luck and were being driven to a remote location to be robbed and, quite possibly, killed. My fears were soon allayed when the resort appeared in the distance and we saw that we were indeed being taken to our destination via a shorter route.

Although this resort was luxurious, it felt about a million times better than it was due to the conditions we had been originally placed in. We were able to eat in a different restaurant each night and sample some weird and wonderful plates of food. A particular highlight for me was the various exotic meats on offer, such as impala and zebra, whereas the downsides were the tripe (overcooked and second only to deep-fried calf brains as the worst thing that I've ever tasted) and the fillet of warthog (without doubt the toughest, chewiest fillet of meat I have ever eaten).

As the testing drew to a close, we were finding a few issues but nothing too major. For me, one of the biggest issues we faced had no impact on the company's financial controls. It was having to deal with a woman in the debtors department who was openly racist, in spite of the presence of a number of black colleagues in the open-plan office that they shared. This made all three of us quite uncomfortable and put us in a difficult position of not knowing whether to bring this to the attention of Otis (himself a black man). In the end, we didn't, putting it down to a difference in cultures, but that decision certainly wasn't sitting comfortably with me, and I suspected that Olive and Aled felt the same.

On one of our last days, we were invited to attend a braai that was being held for the whole workforce as a thank you for their hard work and as a team-building exercise. A braai is a South African barbeque with various meats and a carbohydrate known as mealiepap, which is a traditional porridge/polenta dish that is full of energy but does suffer from a lack of flavour. We felt welcome and enjoyed ourselves, but we were forced to end our stay prematurely, as we were finding ourselves up against the deadline of completing the testing and preparing a closing report to present to Otis and his team.

The closing meeting, where we detailed our findings, went OK. Otis wasn't particularly pleased with some of our findings and argued his corner, as I would expect him to. However, we parted on good terms, and Bruce drove us for the final time as we headed for the airport and our flight home.

The advantages of flying first class were again apparent, as Olive was able to house Ged in the coat closet; surely the first time a sculpted wooden giraffe had had the pleasure of turning left on an airplane. On arrival at Heathrow, I was able to grab a shower and some breakfast before my driver arrived to take me back to my apartment. The change in hemispheres became immediately apparent once I stepped out into the cold November morning, but I quickly forgot about that because I spent the journey home reminiscing about one of the greatest experiences of my life.

CHAPTER 12

From South to West, Illness, and "Retirement"

My secondment in the South ended up lasting almost two years before I was faced with a decision to make regarding my career. Did I want to carry on in my current role and formally relocate to the area permanently or look to relocate to another part of the wider business? The third option was to leave the company completely for pastures new, but that thought never really occurred to me. The company had been good to me and had afforded me some fantastic opportunities. It was also a large enough company to mean that my career options would be quite varied and possibly be international in terms of scope, should I want them to be.

As much as I was enjoying the role, the prospects for this area of the business were beginning to look a little bleak. New orders were proving hard to come by, our bids were proving to be expensive compared to our competitors, and the quality of our present work did not seem to justify the higher prices that were being submitted to our customers. The option of returning to the North had disappeared with news of the closure of the site that was still technically my home office at this stage.

I took the decision to start investigating what my options were outside of my current role.

I looked extensively at the possibilities that might be available in both North America and the Middle East. I favoured North America, as it is somewhere I always enjoy visiting, but the Middle East was definitely something different to what I had experienced so far in my career, and the tax advantages of such a move had not escaped my notice either. I was put in touch with a couple of individuals with experience of working at our Middle East office; they spoke positively of their time out there but were also keen that I understood that the cultural differences were very obvious and that I should not be surprised by anything I witnessed. In the end, the right opportunity never materialised for me, but I had been quite prepared to make that move. The North American opportunities were also proving to be beyond my reach, as the vast majority of the available roles required the successful candidate to be an American citizen, whilst those that didn't were quite junior positions which, on paper, I appeared to be overqualified for.

During this time, I was officially put at risk of redundancy as part of the process of closing the site in the North; however, one of the positive aspects of this was that it allowed me to access the internal job vacancies ahead of their availability to all employees on the company website. One such opportunity was in the company's site in the West. It was similar to the role I was doing, but it would mean working in a much more dynamic area of the business and appeared to offer a much brighter future than my current one. Having applied for the role, I was invited for an interview which would take place within a couple of weeks. I cleared this with my manager, who, whilst showing disappointment at my obvious desire to move on, was very supportive.

On the day before the interview, I left the office early and drove west. I'd booked a cheap and not-so-cheerful hotel room for the evening, the idea being that I could be fully prepared and fresh for the interview rather than making a stupid o'clock commute and running the risk of car problems or the motorway traffic throwing a spanner in the works.

Having used the evening before to carry out a check of where the site was and discovered the best route to get there, I arrived for the interview in plenty of time. Two women who seemed nice and made what looked like extensive notes interviewed me. I felt it had gone well and, without wanting to build my hopes up, felt I had done enough to justify a second interview. Again, my gut instinct proved correct, and a few days later, I was asked to return for a second interview; this time it would be with only one of the women from the first interview and her manager.

For the second interview, I maintained the same routine as previously, even booking the same grim hotel as before in the hope that it was sort of lucky charm (believe me, it would be the only charm I would suggest was attached to the place). The interview panned out the way I had expected in that the senior manager wanted to meet me and get a sense that I was someone he could work alongside and who he thought would fit in with the rest of the team.

They seemed to receive talk of my cooking skills positively, and things were definitely going well. One of the questions I asked was whether they could recommend some areas where I could live if I was fortunate to be offered the job. I quickly altered this to an enquiry as to which areas they *wouldn't* recommend as far as living. They actually went to the trouble of drawing me a map which highlighted both the good and bad areas in the region that I could focus on should I find myself house hunting (the bad areas were emphasised in red ink, which ensured that I got the message loud and clear to avoid these areas at all costs). I took some huge positives out of how well I felt the interview had gone and the fact that they were keen to ensure that I took the bespoke map back down to the South with me.

A few days later, I was in a workshop in London when I received a call to say that I had been offered the role. I was both delighted and relieved that I had managed to stay with the company and move to a new and exciting part of the business. My friends and family were all pleased for me, and my manager was pleased despite the fact that I would be moving on. I set about the task of sourcing a new home and arranging removals ahead of my start date. This was proving a little problematic because workwise I was currently spreading myself incredibly thin. At one point, I calculated that for the best part of the previous six months, I had been at the desk of my main office for a whole week only once, having split my time between the North, the South, the Midlands, London, and our head office as part of my current role. There was also the special task I had become involved in to develop a new risk management system that would be rolled out in, amongst others, my new business unit.

I found a gap in my calendar that allowed me to spend a cold and miserable January weekend in the West, attending as many property viewings as possible in the numerous positive locations that had been pointed out to me at the interview. As in the case of my apartment in the South, a clear favourite emerged from the properties I looked at, and we struck a deal. It was another apartment, and the rental price was similar to what I was paying in the South, but I would be clearly getting much more for my money in the West. The location was close to what would be my new site and was located in a quaint little town rather than a large city. There was a nice-looking bar on one side of me and a church on the other. I imagined myself spending more time in one than the other.

The day soon arrived for me to wave goodbye to my home, job, friends, and colleagues in the South before heading west to begin a new chapter in my life. My last day in the office was a Friday. I arrived late, as I was overseeing the removal firm emptying my apartment as well as ensuring that they had the correct new address for the move the next morning. My manager presented me with a card and some beautiful framed pictures of the area as a leaving gift and as a thank you for all of the cakes and other food that I had brought into the office during my time there.

I gave a brief thank-you speech and explained that I would miss the office and the people but would definitely not miss the traffic, which I explained made me as frustrated as a man who owned a fork in a world of nothing but soup (I'm paraphrasing Noel Gallagher of Oasis with this quote). The traffic situation in the area was without doubt the worst I had ever experienced outside of a capital city. I lived barely ten miles from the office, but it would regularly take around forty-five minutes or more to complete the journey. On one occasion, I foolishly left at the height of rush hour, and I noticed that it took over an hour and a quarter before I reached home. Such was the slowness of the commute that I was able to count the number of traffic lights that I had to negotiate on the route (astonishingly, it was twenty-seven!). I spent the remainder of that Friday and early Saturday morning ensuring the apartment was spotless ahead of returning the keys to the landlady. With everything complete, I headed up the motorway to my new home.

After picking up the keys and meeting with the removal guys, I set about moving in. My parents were due down later that day to lend a hand and have a look around the area I would now be living in. My first impression on entering the apartment was how grotty the placed looked compared to my last visit, and it was obvious that the effort I had put in at my former home had not been replicated here. When my parents arrived, they found me knee-deep in cleaning products, trying to make the place habitable. By the end of the evening, all three of us were totally exhausted, having cleaned the whole apartment from top to bottom and boxed up most of the apartment's furnishings due to their horrendous condition.

Despite it being my first night in a strange bed, sleep came easily because of all the effort I'd put into cleaning. I awoke at exactly 8.30 the next morning. I recall this because it was an unscheduled awakening caused by the church bells ringing! How my brain hadn't made the connection at the time I first viewed the property that the church would obviously have bells that would ring on Sunday mornings is beyond me, and I was currently cursing this oversight. Over the sound of the bells, I could hear my parents doing the same, particularly because Sunday was pretty much the only day of the week that they didn't have to set their alarm clock.

The following day was the first in my new office, so I had to wait until lunch before I could tackle the letting agent regarding the poor condition of my new home. The agent assured me that a team of cleaners had been employed to clean the property prior to my arrival. At times like this, my sarcasm levels tend to go stratospheric and my dark sense of humour has a tendency to come to the fore, as the letting agent was about to find out. "Listen, either you are lying to me or you have employed a team of cleaners who are about as much use as Muhammad Ali's buckaroo set! I have photos on my phone that I took when I first arrived, which prove the property had the look of a Syrian refugee camp, and I want to know exactly what you plan to do about it."

It later transpired that no team of cleaners had been sent and that the previous tenant had left unexpectedly, owing thousands of pounds in debts to pretty much everyone. I eventually received payment for the expense of the cleaning products I had to buy to make the apartment habitable, and a carpet cleaner paid a visit to the apartment. Not long after this, another company bought the agency, and they wasted no time in dispensing with the services of most of the existing staff, including the agent I had dealt with.

My new role was proving to be a bit of a culture shock compared to my previous one; the job role was similar in many ways but I wasn't used to having the whole of my project team on my site and within walking distance. Previously, my role involved a lot of telephone and video conferences and driving to and from other sites around the country. Initially, I was still travelling to London and the head office as part of my role in creating the risk management system. Whilst my participation in this wasn't greatly accepted by my new manager, it was allowed to continue because it was to be implemented in my business unit; therefore, I would be on hand to assist with any initial problems that might arise.

Heading towards my first year end with the business, I noticed that I was starting to struggle to find the motivation to tackle a workday. I was also falling out of love with my exercise regime and becoming increasingly lethargic. My intake of alcohol and convenience foods was also increasing. What I didn't know at this point was that these were the initial warning signs that things were not at all well with regards to my mental health. I spent almost the entire Christmas break splitting my time between my girlfriend's home, her parents' home, and visiting the North to clear out the home I owned there and ensure that it was ready for the imminent sale.

A few days after returning to work after the New Year, I felt terrible. It had taken a great effort to get out of bed and dress myself for work that morning, and now that I was in the office, I was struggling to function properly. I spent a lot of time, amongst other duties, battling with an accounting entry that I was being told had been continuously completed incorrectly. I seemed to have spent almost half of my time that week reversing and re-reversing the same entry as various reporting colleagues advised of the correct treatment to take (this is commonly known as "hokey cokey accounting", as in the song, as you are constantly putting the entry in and then taking it out).

On hearing that the entry would indeed have to be removed yet again, something inside me just snapped. I want to the toilet and locked myself inside a cubicle for the better part of ten minutes, hoping to regain my composure and get a grip of the fact that I was suffering from an overwhelming feeling that I was drowning and struggling to breathe.

Eventually, I went and found my manager and asked if I could talk to her for a few minutes. When she asked if I was OK, I replied no and said that I didn't feel that I could stay in the office a moment longer. She agreed and recommended that I pay a visit to a nearby walk-in clinic in order to get myself checked out.

When I explained the reason for my visit, the doctor advised me to rest and gave me some diazepam to help me sleep. She also instructed me to register with a doctor's surgery in the area (as I was still registered in the North), as I would need to be fully assessed and prescribed further medication.

When I called my parents and my girlfriend and explained the situation, they were not surprised at all. They knew I had been struggling. I took the pills I had been prescribed and went to bed. I've never been the sort of person to take medication of any kind willingly, and I had to be persuaded by the doctor to accept the diazepam. The fact that she had stressed how reluctant she was normally to prescribe the medication highlighted to me how ill I had become without noticing.

I slept better than I had for some time but remember waking up once or twice, which completely freaked me out, as I thought I had taken sleeping pills rather than a relaxant. All I remember thinking was, *Shit, how ill am I that I can't sleep even with the help of tablets?* My new doctor was quick to point out that this was normal and not something I needed to worry about. Her diagnosis of me was that I was suffering from a combination of stress, anxiety, and depression and that I would be required to begin a course of antidepressants as well as beta blockers to counteract the anxiety. She also put me on four weeks' sick leave initially, in the hope that the number of plates that I had been spinning – work, house sale, and divorce, amongst others – would at least decrease.

I spent the next few months convalescing, mainly at my girlfriend's home, returning to my apartment only to attend doctor appointments and the counselling sessions that my company had arranged for me. Staying at my girlfriend's meant that she could keep a close eye on me and ensured that my family and friends in the North would worry less knowing that I was being looked after.

I was still very restless and distracted in the early weeks; the antidepressants didn't seem to be making much difference, and I eventually received a different type. The smallest of things could send me into a deep depression. I remember once making a bolognese sauce for dinner that became too watery, and this was enough to ruin the rest of the day for me. No amount of persuasion from my girlfriend could rectify the situation or make me feel less of a failure.

I have always been my own harshest critic and would allow the tiniest problem to demolish my already brittle self-confidence, and my condition at this time just seemed to magnify these flaws in my character. Even a holiday didn't seem to improve my mental state as much as I would have expected it to, although the fact that there was some skiing involved was not helpful. I had never been keen to try skiing, but my girlfriend loved it, so I thought I would try it. I didn't enjoy it at all and even ended up having a panic attack during the drive to attend one of my skiing lessons before we went on the holiday. I had another similarly bad episode whilst in the gondola heading towards the slopes. The anxiety was heightened further by my fear of heights. I spent the remainder of the skiing trip in bars or wandering the town whilst my girlfriend enjoyed the slopes in a way that I never could.

Whilst I was recuperating, I wanted to begin to tackle an issue that I had allowed to happen, due to my illness, which was that Tracey and I were no longer on speaking terms. I had become more and more distant from both her and her fiancé, Mike. She was obviously very happy with Mike, but for some reason, I wasn't as happy for her as I should have been, which was clearly upsetting Tracey. With hindsight, what appeared to be a selfish attitude on my part in not appearing interested in Tracey being so happy was clearly another warning sign that I was beginning to shut myself down mentally with people who I really cared about and who cared about me.

We had arranged a meetup one weekend when my girlfriend and I were visiting the North; I had restricted the meeting to about three hours, which Tracey was not happy about, so it ended up not happening. We then had no contact of any kind for the better part of six months. Looking back, I think my behaviour was driven by an inner fear that Tracey was smart enough to know that something wasn't quite right with me and that the relationship I had with my then-girlfriend was not as good as I was telling myself it was. This was me avoiding tackling issues head-on and putting things off instead. I had been doing it for some time with my divorce and also the sale of my house, blaming work commitments for the delay, when, in reality, I was deliberately burying myself into more and more work to justify my behaviour to myself – and now I was doing it with some of my closest friends.

One day I was having a coffee in Liverpool when Tracey sent me an email. She explained that she missed me and loved me and hoped that I would respond. I thought about how I should reply to Tracey's email. There was no doubt that I would reply, as it had become obvious that I had missed Tracey as much as she had missed me. Over the next few days, we exchanged messages and started to work towards getting our relationship back to that of surrogate brother and sister, eventually meeting up with her and Mike and introducing her to my girlfriend. I apologised to them both for how I had behaved over the previous twelve months or so and assured them that I was beginning to feel much better thanks to the medication and my counselling sessions.

The counselling provided by my employer was indeed a great help to me; it allowed me to talk over all of my issues with someone totally independent but who was also able to act as devil's advocate and ask the awkward questions that I knew I needed to answer. The sessions were about an hour long, and I never once found myself short of things to discuss or looking at my watch to see how much time remained before the session was over. I embraced the counselling rather than being sceptical of it, which undoubtedly meant that I got much more from it than I otherwise might have.

I remember one session where the counsellor and I disagreed about the subject of my new-found mentality. For years, I had been incredibly fastidious, especially when it came to managing my finances. As you might expect from an accountant, I would be meticulous when reviewing my monthly credit card statement, ensuring I had a receipt for every entry on there, but I was now finding myself giving each statements a cursory glance and, if it looked about right, simply paying the balance. The counsellor felt that this was progress, saying, "Sometimes good enough is good enough." I was at the opposite end of this opinion and was actually worrying about my more relaxed attitude to personal finance, arguing that "good enough is good enough" was something totally alien to someone as self-critical of themselves as I was and that, in my view, this was more "Sod it; that will do". This went back and forth for at least five minutes, until we agreed to disagree and moved on. However, to be fair to the counsellor, I am still not as meticulous as I was previously, although I do ensure that I have a reasonable recollection of each transaction and don't feel that I am cutting any corners by doing this.

Eventually, I felt ready to begin thinking about going back to work; a phased return was constructed to bring me back into the working environment slowly, building myself up into a full-time role again over a period of weeks, which would include regular reviews with both my doctor and my employers. Everyone on the team was pleased to see me back, and I brought some sweet and savoury goodies into the office that I had made to say thanks for their patience and understanding.

Unfortunately, after about six weeks I suffered a relapse and again found myself struggling to overcome the anxiety attacks that had crippled me previously. The main reason for this was that the paperwork for the divorce had been rejected due to an error on my part, for there was a section I hadn't completed. This one small oversight was enough to send me back to square one in my rehabilitation. My confidence was again at rock bottom, and more importantly the divorce, one of the key issues that I had avoided for so long, seemed determined to hang over me for some time to come.

Eventually, the paperwork was rectified and accepted, so I began the process of working towards another phased return to the office, but by this time, I was having to take sleeping tablets the evening before a workday to ensure I got some rest as well as beta blockers before going to work to help with the anxiety. This was in addition to the antidepressants I was already taking daily for the foreseeable future. A couple of months passed, and I finally built myself up into working full weeks again. It had taken longer than I had hoped, but I was finally there, and it seemed that a sense of normality was returning to my life; unfortunately, I was wrong.

My relationship with my girlfriend had begun showing some signs of not being particularly healthy of late. Initially, I had put this down to the strain of my illness and the toll it had inevitably taken on the relationship, but there were other issues presenting themselves, which once again I had buried myself away from or ignored in the hope that they would just disappear. The main issues were her desire for marriage and children, which I had failed to dampen or even attempt to address during the year or so that we had been together. It hadn't proved to be a problem in the beginning, as those were the early days and there was no guarantee of the relationship being long term. But as time went on, I broached neither subject, so my girlfriend clearly felt that it was only a matter of time before both things became a reality.

The fact that I had begun divorce proceedings from my wife must have been seen as further proof that a proposal was about to be made. By the time the decree nisi had been confirmed, I decided to make by position of not wanting to be part of another marriage clear. This was not greatly received by my girlfriend, although she did admit that she had started to get the feeling that I would not want to enter into another marriage given the fact that my first wedding was for mainly pragmatic reasons rather than the usual reasons.

The conversation quickly moved to my thoughts on starting a family, and finally I had to admit that it was something I had never felt the need to fulfil. I then received an ultimatum: either I agreed to begin a family or we would have to go our separate ways. I asked for some time to consider this and went away for the better part of a week to think things through. I spent my time considering the ultimatum and drawing up a list of pros and cons to ensure that I made the correct decision concerning my future.

Having been unwell for most of the relationship, in part without knowing it, I had been blind to what most of my family and friends had noticed, and that was that my girlfriend and I were two very different people wanting very different things out of life. I arranged to meet her at her house to talk further; I had made the decision that the relationship was over, so I ensured that my car contained any belongings of hers from the apartment before driving over to deliver the news. Understandably, she was upset despite half expecting the worst. She left to visit a friend and give me time to collect my things. She insisted that we were to have no contact in the future, but we wished each other well before she left.

Whilst the decision to end the relationship was mine, it still hit me quite hard, and inevitably I found myself off work again as a result. Luckily, I had two weeks holiday coming up so I could take off somewhere and regroup before preparing myself to return to the office.

On my return, I again embarked on a phased return initially before building up towards working full weeks again. I was confident that a corner had been turned, for despite my relationship ending, most of the issues that had caused my illness had been put to bed. The house was sold, the divorce was complete, and my stress levels at work were being managed.

One morning I found myself again gripped by anxiety and unable to get out of bed, the covers feeling like an iron blanket that couldn't be moved, whilst it also felt as if a sumo wrestler was seated on my chest with no plans to relocate himself anytime soon. Once again, I found myself back at the start of my rehabilitation, but the frustrating thing this time was that there was no obvious trigger for why it had occurred. I was doing all the right things to ensure my recovery was continuing, but it had made no difference, for some reason. I found myself back at the doctor and on sick leave yet again; a cycle then began in which I would gear myself up for a return to work, only to find myself crippled by anxiety on the morning I was due to return.

After several weeks of this, I made the decision that it was perhaps time for me to re-evaluate things and consider the possibility of resigning from my job. I was taking two to three different types of medication just to get me through a working day, and the thought of potentially having to do this for the rest of my life was not a prospect that I felt I could accept. It was also unfair to my employer, who had been incredibly supportive throughout my illness, and I felt I was continuously letting people down by insisting that I was ready to return but finding myself held back by anxiety on every occasion.

A meeting was arranged with my manager to allow us to discuss things. We reached an agreement, and I gave my resignation there and then, drawing up a brief letter to formalise things. I thanked my manager for the support I had received and requested that my best wishes as well as the news that I would not be returning be passed on to the rest of the team.

After twenty years of full employment and a proud record of never being unemployed, I now found myself without a job, yet I was remarkably relaxed about the situation. I was lucky enough to be in the situation where making such a decision was not going to affect anyone else, for I had no real commitments, such as children. I also knew that I had a skill to fall back on that was always in demand should I be unable to find a more suitable career for myself or if I needed to support myself financially in the future. But this would be a last resort for me, as I have to admit that accountancy has never been a true calling. It was always a means to an end that allowed me to visit some fantastic destinations, eat in some of the world's best restaurants, and lavish my friends and family with luxury gifts.

In fact, I am very much a black sheep of the accountancy fraternity, many of whom are joked about as being so mean that they won't exhale or even defecate, as it seems that they are parting with something for free. I possess an antipathy of people who illustrate such behaviour. After all, we are a long time dead and life is surely for living. I'm proud of the fact that I have never required an overdraft or been in debt other than that of a mortgage or personal loan, but no matter how frugal you are with money, you cannot take it with you when you die.

I remember being on the end of one of the usual "You're an accountant so you must be mean" jibes during my time in the South, and I responded by describing myself as being similar to a doctor who smoked, with spending money being my unlikely vice, given my profession, rather than the doctor's nicotine addiction. I hope this book has gone some way to proving this to be true and that any prejudices you may have had towards accountants beforehand have been softened somewhat by the tales that you have read in these pages.

25733312R00072

Printed in Great Britain
by Amazon